Tempus ORAL HISTORY *Series*

Clay Country
voices

A china clay pit, 1973.

Tempus ORAL HISTORY Series

Clay Country
voices

Compiled by
Mike Turner

TEMPUS

First published 2000
Copyright © Mike Turner, 2000

Tempus Publishing Limited
The Mill, Brimscombe Port,
Stroud, Gloucestershire, GL5 2QG

ISBN 0 7524 2078 X

Typesetting and origination by
Tempus Publishing Limited
Printed in Great Britain by
Midway Clark Printing, Wiltshire

The flesh that is clay, the open-cast mine
Where men are not trapped but work with the wind on their faces.
Jack Clemo

The railway viaduct, St Austell.

Contents

Acknowledgements

Most of the photographs were supplied by those who contributed to this book, or were taken by Mike Turner. The exceptions are attributed in the text by the initials of the appropriate organization, as follows:

WMM: St Austell China Clay Museum, Wheal Martyn
RCM: The Royal Cornwall Museum, Truro
GVL: Goonvean Ltd, St Stephen
EN: English Nature

In addition I thank Joy Payne for allowing me to use the recordings she made of Blanche Williams; Pauline Sweet for the map of the clay area on pages 64 and 65 and the publishers Bloodaxe for permission to use the quotation from Jack Clemo – who used to live in a cottage, still standing, near Treviscoe. I am also grateful for permission to print photographs of the railway carriage homes, both inhabited and derelict, by the owners of these interesting structures.

An old chimney at Bowling Green, with ivy and foxgloves.

Introduction

You think of Cornwall, you think of holidays, the astonishingly beautiful coastline, cliffs and coves and deep blue water. But, historically, the county has always been industrialized, particularly in the centre and west where the land was rich in metallic ores and in china clay deposits. From the eighteenth century onwards, Cornwall throbbed with the rhythm of huge beam engines pumping water from mine and open cast pit, hauling minerals, clay and waste materials to the surface. In addition, much of the manufacture of the heavy machinery was done in nearby foundries and workshops.

Around the coast in hundreds of harbours, people made a living from the pilchard industry, catching, processing, packing and transporting the fish. And from the bright green fields on the downs above the wooded river valleys, farmers reared the cows that gave the milk that produced the clotted cream Cornwall became famous for.

Betjeman thought it was a pretty good place to be, and a thousand thousand city-sad holidaymakers in their chalets and caravan tin-towns still agree. But the guts have been torn out of Cornwall. The fishing fleet has dwindled, the farmers are in deep trouble and since research on

A clay pit. A monitor (high pressure hose) can be seen washing clay out from the cliff-face in the background. [RCM]

The 'Cornish Alps' from the St Stephen to Bugle road.

this book began the last tin mine closed down. The tourist are still here though. They crowded in in 1999 to see the eclipse, which came and went in a couple of hundred seconds – after which they all sighed, packed away their darkened glasses and slowly gridlocked themselves away.

But we cannot all live on service industries. Somewhere, somebody has to be producing goods, creating wealth – or at the very least maintaining subsistence. In Cornwall the heart beats on appropriately in the very centre of the county: clay country. This book takes the pulse of the clay country. Who lives there? Who works there? Who *used* to work there? Is the heart healthy? Changing its rhythm? If so, why? And how?

During the last two years of the millennium I cycled round the clay area, talking to whoever would agree to speak into the microphone of my mini-disc recorder. Many were former clay industry workers. Some still work in the clay. But others were farmers, postmen, train drivers, students, local politicians, conservationists.... The sweep was as large as I could make it in the time I had set myself for completion of the task. Many of them are represented in this book, but not all. To include everyone who spoke to me would take a volume about ten times the size of this.

To describe fully the way clay is extracted from the ground would take another book several times the size of this, but for readers unfamiliar with clay country and its working methods, the following brief description may be helpful.

China clay is white. It is decomposed granite – the same granite which can be seen in outcrops on Bodmin Moor, for instance. It lies below the topsoil, but near enough to the surface to be reached by open-cast mining. Great expanses of the area shown on the map on pages 64 and 65 have been hollowed out, ulcerated by gigantic pits. The clay is washed out. A high-pressure jet of water is played upon the cliff-face of the pit, and this washes a white stream of china clay down to the pit floor, from where it is pumped away back to the surface for drying to a powder, removal of waste materials such as mica, and blending. These days most china clay is not used for the production of china at all, but for producing the thin white film on the surface of this paper, for instance. There are hundreds of other industrial uses, well documented elsewhere.

Apart from the holes in the ground, the main impact on the landscape of central Cornwall has been the piles of waste – the Cornish Alps, so called because of their conical shape and white appearance. As every gravedigger knows, where you have a hole you have a mound, and the huge Cornish holes make huge Cornish mounds – and the industry has always been anxious, some might say desperate, to find space to create more mountains of waste. Fields were lost, houses were buried, villages vanished underground. For many years people tolerated this necessary consequence of the way they earned their bread and butter.

Not so now. Times have changed. The industry has changed – small family firms have been amalgamated into larger industrial complexes, and now most of the china clay industry of mid-Cornwall is concentrated in the body of one multinational leviathan, Imerys.

Part of this story is told in the following pages – the part which affected the lives of the clay workers who spoke to me. But it is only a part. As an oral historian I rely wholly on what people choose to tell me. This is not a book of social science or economics. It is a collection of stories told by a selection of Cornish storytellers at the end of the twentieth century – so some extracts are included simply because the speaker had a good tale to tell. I like a good yarn. I hope you do too.

John Keay House, headquarters of ECC (now Imerys), St Austell.

A NOTE ON THE FORMAT

Each extract is identified by either the speaker's name at the beginning of the extract, or his/her initials at the end. 'Charlie' and 'Bob' are pseudonyms. I have not tried too hard to indicate the dialect of a speaker, except by a few phonetic spellings. Extensive phonetic rendering of any accent is never successful and usually unreadable. All my introductory and explanatory text is printed in italics. My questions during the interviews are preceded by a dash.

COMPANY NAMES

The major clay company until 1999 was ECC (English China Clays – more accurately ECC International). Most of the contributors use either this name or ECLP (English Clays, Lovering, Pochin) an older name for what was the amalgamation of a multiplicity of small clay companies. More recently ECC has been taken over by Imerys, a multinational organization based in Paris.

Entering clay country at St Austell.

10

CHAPTER 1

Schooldays: Work and Play

Hensbarrow, with its Bronze Age tumulus overshadowed by a waste tip, summer 2000. The hill is around 1000ft above sea level.

School Life

There follow three short accounts of school life, spanning the first sixty years of this century. First is Bob....
—*Did your father start in the clay straight from school?*

You started at school, and when you'd done the work of the year you got turned up, irrespective of whether it had taken the year. So the brighter people in the school ended up in Standard VII at eleven, twelve, thirteen, but had to stay on until they was fourteen. So when his turn come, father was one of these that got into Standard VII a bit ahead of time and spent eighteen months, or whatever it was, helping the headmaster out in teaching the others.

I can't ever remember more than one

person that couldn't read and write, and he was a mongol. He used to come to school perhaps once or twice a term, when he felt like it. He died in his early teens, as most did then. [He] would turn up sometimes, much to the amazement of all the rest of us, and do more or less what he liked. He amazed me because he would get on the bus, and ride over to his place without paying. I couldn't imagine how the policeman never took him off to prison. They knew that he wasn't wired up right. Bus drivers and conductors knew him, and they would stop outside his place. There was no stop there really, but the bus driver would stop and let him off. I've known him turn up at school and be a bloody nuisance really. Everybody put up with it and jollied him along – there was nothing much you could do about it. He was only waiting to die. Things were different then. Life felt different.

Central and western Cornwall were unusual in having an educational establishment, the Camborne School of Mines, which provided an escape route for working-class children – presumably only boys – from the working class to professional or skilled status. This is Laurie Stuthridge....

I was fortunate enough to get a scholarship to the local grammar school. Did five years, took School Certificate, didn't know what I wanted to do so went into the sixth form. I was obviously not interested in the arts. It was science – maths and science. Mines and minerals came into it, because any spare time we had, which wasn't much, we'd be scratching around old mine workings, collecting mineral specimens. Now you can imagine, an ordinary working man with a seventeen-year-old son – and school leaving age in those days was fourteen – occasionally he'd say, 'Well, have you decided yet, son, what you want to do?' 'No, dad.'

I can remember now, sitting in class in school, and one of the prefects came around with a huge notice, and it was advertising Cornwall County Scholarships to the Camborne School of Mines. It was like a flash of lightning. That is what I wanted to do. So when I went home that evening – and I can still picture the situation – there was Mum and Dad sitting down at the table, and I walked in. Dad looked at me and it must have been obvious because he said, 'Well, son, what have you decided?' And I said to him, 'I want to go to the School of Mines, at Camborne.' His face fell. He said, 'Son, there's no way that we can afford to pay – and you must realize that.' I said, 'Yes, I do. But what's triggered it is this advert for scholarships, with a contribution towards an extra grant for digs and lodgings.' So he said, 'Well if you can' – looking at Mum at the same time – 'I suppose we've kept you this long – if you can get a scholarship and you can perhaps, in between times, earn enough money to provide for your books and your lodgings, we can probably keep you in clothes, keep you as we have done.' I said, 'Right!' I got a scholarship, and that's what started me off at the School of Mines.

Like most clay country children, Laurie had extra-curricular tasks to do.

I had to go each morning before I went to school twice to the tap, which was about 200, 250 yards away, with two 2-gallon buckets. I had to get enough water for the house, and for the washing; for our own needs plus the needs of the animals. That was eight gallons of water in the morning,

Bugle, with a clay tip in background, in 1999.

same again in the evenings. No street lights in that area. Weekends used to bug me a bit. The only means of getting hot water for washing – well here they used to call it a copper but it's cast iron, with a fire underneath. I had to get enough water over a Saturday and Sunday to fill this thing. I can't remember for the life of me how many buckets it took, but it took an awful lot.

Friday evenings and Saturday mornings I used to work at the local butcher's. Friday evenings, usually it was spent making sausages. Everything had to be done by turning this handle. You fed the skins on the end, you turned this handle. Before that you had to mix the sausage mix, and that was all done by hand, so it was quite hard work. Saturday morning, it would be delivering meat on the old-fashioned bicycle with a basket on the front. The butcher doing his rounds during the week would take the weekend orders from local people, and the Saturday morning yours truly would be out on the bike delivering the orders. It was worthwhile because at the end of it I used to get a couple of bob and a piece of meat for the weekend. Meat was rationed, but then, once you're up working with the butcher you're on the inside track!

Les Lean lived in one of the highest parts of the area – almost 1000ft above sea level.

Oh yeah. I used to go to school – I been up Hensbarrow hill – used to go to Roche school see, from up there – over the top, down over Hensbarrow Hill. Sometimes it used to be so windy, going up there, used to have to walk backwards; couldn't breathe hardly. When snow, couldn't walk down the road, had to walk up on the bank around. I

13

was up there last week trying to pick some urts [i.e. 'hurts' or 'whorts', bilberries or whortleberries]. When we was going to school we used to pick them all the time in jam jars – pick these urts, have urt tart.

Childhood Games

In the forties, children seemed to be enviably free from restrictions and the fear of molestation. It was a small, and perhaps somewhat conservative (in the best sense) community. Here is Bob....

In the days of my youth a branch line encircled Bugle, with a main crossroads going through the middle of the village. Three of those roads were cut off by the branch line looping around it, the one going north to Bodmin and the one going west to Roche and the one going south to St Austell were all crossed by that branch line. So that was three bridges. The other road was crossed by a bridge from a clay works, hauling sand to a tip on the opposite side of the road from the pit.

So really there were four bridges around Bugle, two or three hundred yards from the Square. Our territory, when we went out to play in the dark, would be 'don't go outside the bridges' – which meant you had the run of the village for hide and seek, and kick the tin, and eek-squeak-whistle and hollo, and all the nonsense we used to play.

—What's eek-squeak-whistle?

One person would be a chaser and the rest run away, and he would shout, 'Eek, squeak, whistle or hollo!' You had to either go 'eek', or 'hollo', depending how far away you were, to give him some idea of where he was searching. Of course if you was in the bush right behind where he was standing, you eeked. If you was 500 yards away, you could hollo. There was no idea that anybody you met could possibly do you any harm, physical, moral, spiritual or any other way. They wouldn't have lasted long if they did. The village policed itself to a large extent. Everybody was known to everybody else – although when I was early teenage was during the war, in which case there was evacuees around. But they settled into the same pattern of things. They were queer buggers when they came, because they were East Enders from Paddington and places like that. But hadn't been there for six or twelve months before they was village children, really. They'd taken on the lifestyle of the people they were billeted with. They'd never seen a cow, or never seen the sea – and some of them never even seen a bloody bath before! [He laughs.] So they were a bit different from us when they came. Probably because we was a Celtic community, they came in and they could take us or leave us, suit themselves. There's welcome if they could fit in, and if they couldn't fit in they could bugger off to London and be bombed, they could suit theirself.

Before the war we played on the burrows. During the war most of the clay works shut down through shortage of labour and shortage of markets. It meant that they became playgrounds for us – catching minnows in two-pound jam pots with string, skating on them in the hard winters that we had, picking blackberries, and bird's-nesting. One toy that we made – because pre-war a lot of clay went out in barrels, in casks – there were a number of barrel staves on the works. Get into a shed and find that there might be 500 barrel staves in there. So you would pick one each, and fabricate a seat to go on the back, and a cross bar on the front, and a bit of string. Take it to the top of a burrow and sit on it and down you go – thirty degree angle of repose, and the sand is hard once it's been left for a few years. You go down there like hell through Italy, and then whistle out through the withy bushes at the bottom for a braking system.

I used to laugh – a captain worked for me, older boy than myself. When he became a clay work captain and I was his manager he was very hot on safety, and I used to smirk behind, quietly thinking, 'I can remember you as a big boy coming down over Rocks burrow in a pie dish.' You can imagine, a pie dish on a hard sand surface at thirty degrees reaching nearly terminal velocity, and he's crouched up with a big – oh I don't know – perhaps 18 inches or 2 foot long and a foot wide, a family enamel pie dish. He's sitting with his backside on the back edge and heels tucked in front, and gripping the sides hoping that he won't skin his knuckles.

A conical burrow on a quiet day – no barrel stave toboggans.

…and Laurie Stuthridge:

From the time we were about five, with no toys, we actually had on a piece of waste ground – I suppose today you'd call it a model clay work – but to us it was our work. We had the pit, we had the incline, we used to use strips of wood for the rails. The skip was a self-tipping skip which we made ourselves. The wheels were cotton reels cut in half, so you got the flanges to run on the tracks. And there'd be one or two [children] working in the pit. Another one would be perhaps five yards away, and he'd be the winder, he'd have the winding engine. There'd be a piece of string with a tin and a stone on the end, so you would ring it once to stop, and twice to go down, three to go up

– and it was a working clay pit. We were playing at being at work. There were flooded pits, just as there are now, and – I'm sure our parents would have had kittens had they known, but – we'd find old planks of wood and build a raft. Get out on this – perhaps 100ft of water underneath.

—Terrifying!

Absolutely.

—What did you make the rafts out of?

Oil drums, planks, whatever we could find, and lashed them together. One or two would tip up because someone would be on it, and

15

A raft on a clay-pit pool, at Kneehigh's Hendra pit project 1998 (see also below). The old traditions are still maintained.

Clayton Roberts, summer 2000.

someone else would say, I'm coming on, and get on the side and.... We had no knowledge of boat-building or raft-building. We learnt to swim in the clay processing tanks.

Karslake

Clayton Roberts lived in the now vanished village of Karslake – twenty-four houses on a bleak hillside near Hensbarrow, surrounded by pits and waste tips, or burrows.

We used to have a scramble track around the back where we used to race old cars cut down, just the chassis and the engine. I remember a guy called Johnny Hancock who was always classed as being a hard man. And he was a hard man, a very big bloke, hard bloke. And I was there walking out one day and he said, Come on boy – and he picked me up and put me on the seat of this here jalopy – nothing around you, just the chassis and the engine. He took me out round the track. I come back like a mud ball. He just parked me outside the house and buggered off. My mother went berserk. She'd just washed and polished me and put me out.

Today, people would look at it that we were impoverished, but to me as a child it was a fantastic playground. I never thought that I was restricted in any way because I lived there. I loved it there. You had the freedom to do what you wanted. It didn't matter what age the kids was, we all got on. I can't remember ever having any squabbles. Everybody looked after everybody, and if you were the littlest in the line, then always the older girls looked after you. They always protected you.

—*How many kids lived up there?*

I suppose... I think the Dingles had thirteen kids. I suppose there must have been thirty-five, forty children. There was loads of kids. Dad used to make a go-cart and we always used to have dillies, we used to call them, these little soap box jobbies. We used to put a sail on them. And the wind up there was colossal, you can imagine, so we used to take off and away we used to go. You'd be going by the edge of a pit down the road a bit, and you tried to turn right but the wind was telling you that you was going left. The number of times we've nearly ended up going over the side of a bloody deep pit. We used to go on frog chases. Chase these poor frogs into bloody oblivion. Gangs of us, chasing frogs. You get a frog and then you literally chase it. It hops away from you so you all run after it, trying to stamp on it. Terrible. Terrible things you do when you're children. [We]

used to play in the gorse. You'd get a box of matches [puff...puff...] – there was always fires going on and most of the time kids started them. We used to dig tunnels under peoples garages or sheds. and one went directly under Kitty Dingle's shop – [he laughs] – because there was no foundations. We got caught like that a few times, and pulled out and given a right rollicking, because of the dangers of it, if the bloody thing collapsed.

Par Harbour

Colin Croker lived in St Blazey. The harbour he refers to is Par, the clay-exporting port.

That was your playground. Now, you wouldn't be allowed to, but it was a great playground, fantastic. The harbour was a playground. We swam down in the harbour. When the tide was out you used to have mud races, sliding down in the mud. We didn't know it was polluted like that. A great place to grow up. Those bag slides – they would have conveyor belts and down would come the bags, nearly a hundredweight in weight – well we used to go down those chutes as well. Terrific thing. Just like a theme park. They'd set the things going and we would jump in. We shouldn't have been doing it, but we were young – what twelve, fifteen years of age. As long as you kept out of the way of the trains and the obviously dangerous things, the staff didn't mind. It could be boring for them sometimes, specially on the night shift.

There were – and are – clay dries near the harbour, long sheds where the clay was spread in pans. Underfloor heating dried the wet clay to powder form.

—Could you just walk in to a clay dry then?

Oh yeah, you walk in. They were always glad – the chap who was stoking the fires, he was always glad of somebody to talk to, a couple of teenage boys strolling up, have a yarn. Specially if it was raining and we got wet. Stand in front of the oven – the air would draw you almost in, terrific drawing power. We'd be dry in seconds [he laughs]. Great fun.

An All-Rounder

Tom Browne was a strong youth, good at all sports, and a renowned fighter.
—So you were playing football until you were 36?

Tom Browne in his retirement photograph.

Yes. That was a laugh really. This chap come up. 'Here', he said, 'can you help us out Saturday, playing football?' 'Hell,' I said, 'I told you I was going to hang up my boots.' 'Well,' he said, 'we're a man short and we're playing in the semi-final of the Junior Cup, and I'm hoping that we can win that one.' I said, 'All right.' I got my boots out come the Saturday, and went, and we won. I scored two bloody goals. Beat 'em three to one. Went on to win the Junior Cup, then.

We had a good little [cricket] side for a school team. I was the captain of the team. They batted first and we had em all out for13 runs. I used to send down a fairly fast ball. I took 7 wickets in that match. Course, there was one or two youngsters there – they was afraid of the bloody ball! [He laughs.]

—You frightened them out, did you?

Well no, I skittled 'em out clean. I was opening bat. First ball I had I hit for six, and then a four. We got up to 28 and the master said, 'We'll give you the match'. A county player for Sussex come over afterwards and he said, 'I've a good mind to put your name through for coaching. You got a lovely action with a ball and also you got the shoulders that can drive a ball.' I did, I had big shoulders as a boy of twelve, aye.

—When you were playing for the school team, did you wear whites?

No. Pads was all you had, and the school supplied the bats. Most of us used to manage to get a white shirt to put on. The only [football] kit we had was the football. We'd have a shirt in the green and black colours of St Blazey.

—Did you always manage to buy football boots?

The Hendra Pit Project – raft-builders and village lads.

I borrowed 'em. My mother couldn't afford 'em. My father – they were old people, a little pension of 10s a week in they days. It was a big family too. Ten children.

Hendra Pit

In 1999 Kneehigh Theatre Company worked with local people – and others – to devise an event in a disused clay pit. In fifty years, some attitudes of young people seem not to have changed much. This is Sue Hill.

Every time you drove anywhere a load of kids would jump in the van with you, and you'd have really interesting conversations with these kids. I asked one of the lads, 'What do you reckon to this place then? Is it good living here?' He said, 'It's great living here, it's really great living here.' I said,

'Why's that?' He said, 'Well, there's really good mates and – look around. It's amazing, this place. It's like an enormous playground. Its a fantastic place.' The kids, certainly in that area, think its a cool place to be. And also because it is a bit tough.

There's this huge... they're water storage tanks, settling tanks, but they're right near the road at Hendra. There's one called Tank 9 and it's their swimming pool. You can drive along the road and you can hear this incredible racket. There'll be maybe thirty or forty kids in this tank. It's quite a thing to get into it. You have to climb up a 6ft wall, and then you have to walk across about 15ft of supply pipe – and you're 8 or 9ft off the ground. And the tank itself has got quite sheer sides for getting in and out of the water, so there's the whole thing about it being a bit of an adventure, and it's great for them. There's nothing else there. There's no

Settling tanks in the Melbur area. There's not much water here – mostly wet clay.

youth clubs in that area, there's no drop-in centre or any of the other facilities you might expect if it was a similar situation in an urban centre. But there is a sense in which they kind of do it for themselves.

Heligan

Caroline Smale lived in the fishing port – as it was then – of Mevagissey, on the edge of clay country, and near what is now the Lost Garden of Heligan.

We spent a lot of our childhood, especially fine weather, in Heligan [she puts the stress on the second syllable] woods in the, what they call the lost gardens of Heligan [stress on first syllable] now. We used to pack up just a sandwich or a bottle of lemonade and we'd spend the whole day in Heligan woods, playing hide and seek, building houses in the trees, boys and girls. Never any fear of

anyone being hurt. So long as you came home grubby and muddy about tea time. It was a lovely, lovely lot of young people. Sadly we lost quite a few young men in the war. You don't forget them, do you? It's just boys that you grew up with.

Foxhole Football

Football, clay country-style! Arthur Bullock remembers a famous Foxhole match.

We played Nanpean, when I was going to school, up on the downs – it wasn't a field – we pulled up all old vearns, as we call them [i.e. bracken], and made out goal posts with our coats. We didn't have a football. We found an old case and we stuffed en with straw, and we played a match like that. It was brilliant.

CHAPTER 2

Working in the Clay

Workers at Blackpool Pit, c. 1915 – with their kettle in the foreground. [RCM]

Good Experience

Before the days of Labour Exchanges, finding a job was a more informal procedure. Much use was made of family networks. The fathers – and uncles, and cousins and grandfathers – of many clay district boys were already employed by one or other of the many small companies extracting clay. Bob recalls:

Before I graduated I'd gone up with my father to hold the survey staff. Occasionally

he used to say, 'Boy, cancel anything for tomorrow, I need you for a day.' If he was doing levelling, rather than take a company workman just to stand around holding the staff, he'd say, ''Tis good experience for you, I need you and that's that.' And on I'd trundle – pleased to go with him, because you had the old man's company. We'd eat dinner in a hotel up there together, and for a schoolboy as I was then 'twas a little bit special. I'd get half a shandy – that was really something.

[My father] said, 'Wait in the car, I want to see the manager, Mr Grime.' When he came out he said, 'I don't know what he want but Mr Grime want a word with you, boy. Be respectful.' On I went. When I come out he said, 'What did Frank Grime want?' I said, 'He offered me a job when I graduate.' I was at Camborne then, first or second year. Father said, 'What did 'e say?' I said, 'I thanked him very much for the offer, and I thought about it for a minute and said that I thought that I would go abroad.' He asked me what I had against working in the clay industry. They were recruiting graduates now, which was unusual for them. My reasoning was that if I took the job I'd never know whether he was giving me the job or he was rewarding father for having been a bloody good bloke all these years. I said, 'If I go abroad I shall know whether I'm any good or not, because nobody else will know anything connected with me other than what they see right in front their physog.'

He said '...More damn sense than I thought you had, boy.' So evidently he was pleased.

Clay-work Interviews

A few decades later, John Cloke applied in a more modern way, but with an individualistic twist.

I signed on for the merchant navy when I left school at fourteen. Everybody else was going to work for ECLP, so I took it on my own back to go up to John Keay House and ask for a job. At the time there was 105 applicants for five jobs. I wasn't one of them, of course, but I just asked if there was a chance of a job. They said, While you'm here, yes you can have an interview. I went in and had my interview. I was asked a lot of questions, what I could do, what I couldn't do. I said, I can't do anything, I don't know anything, but I'm prepared to learn everything. Because if I said I could do jobs, I was given a job which I couldn't do, I would make myself look a fool. But I told the truth. I've now left school, I'm now going to start to learn about life. And it just went from there. I was taken on as a works trainee.

Making Ends Meet

When George Morcom left school the whole country was in an economic crisis. Work was scarce, and his family was finding it difficult to make ends meet.

When I left school – 1926 onward – the clay works were in a very bad state. A lot of men were on the dole so they weren't taking any boys on. Schoolmaster said to me, they want a boy in a certain place; you go over there and see if you can get a job. So when I got over to get this job, he said, 'Oh I promised it to one of the men who work here, for his boy.' They was already in. I went three clay works and 'twas all the same, the job was promised to men that was working there.

A local man come in to Mother and he said, 'I've got a job for your boy, in a big garage behind the White Hart' – that was about the first garage. He said, 'They'll waive the premium; he can have half a crown a week.' Mother said, 'That's no good, because the minute he works I shall lose the 5s a week that he's got from the pension book.' My sister would have the 5s, but she was having 3s 6d before. Mother said, 'No. We shall be out of pocket, we can't do that.'

Then he come in another time and said,

'I got another job for your boy, working for the firm in St Austell selling Quaker tea. You go round with the Quaker van to sell the tea to the shops – 8s a week.' Mother said, 'That ain't no good.' Because I was losing 3s 6d, you see, and the 3s 6d my sister would be losing would be 7s. Mother couldn't afford to do that. I eventually got to work for the farmer; 10s 6d a week, working about 60 hours a week.

The Captain

The captain was a foreman. He probably knew not only your father, but many other of your family members who worked in the clay. Between the two of them, they gave Charlie his start in clay work.

[My father] sent me down to see the captain. He knew that there was going to be a vacancy down at Quarry Close. He came home and he sent me up to where the captain's house was. I had to ask for a job, and of course I had to tell him who I was and what I was. He knew my father. I got took on as a kettle boy then.

Tending the Engines

In a time when schooling tended to be brief, it was still possible for a comparatively uneducated young man of good intelligence and strong force of character to make his mark. Bob's father was one such.

His father's cousin was captain and said, 'Send Ralph on. If he's any good we can find a job for a youngster.' In the old days everybody that left school practically went clay work. That was the big employer in the

Captain Tom Yelland. [WMM]

area, and every works had six or eight boys under age. They were only paid a pittance. The idea where you was paid man's wages for doing boy's work is a recent invention. So father went to Treverbyn, and they were putting in two gas engines. The makers had sent down an installation engineer, and Cap'n Wills said, 'Well Ralph, you'd better go on and tend the man from England that's putting in the gas engines.' Father was fairly bright and keen, and had built his own steam engines as a kid out of treacle tins and soldered pipes and bits and pieces. I got an engine up in the loft now that he built when he was a teenager, just after he started work. Anyway, on he went with the maker's man, and the maker's man, away from home with nothing to do more than install the engine and kick his heels, cottoned to him I suppose. They got on very well and he started to show him how to install an engine.

The Apprentice

Twenty-odd years ago, some attempt was made to continue the education of young clayworkers. Clayton Roberts:

[ECC] used to take you on as a trainee pit operative. It was a two-year programme from sixteen years old to eighteen, and basically you go [to] the majority of pits and plants around the company, training on different machinery. They send you for college for a day a fortnight, which was a total and utter waste of time.

—Was that at St Austell college?

The tutors came from the college. We actually done it at Goonbarrow block works. They used to have a little training centre up there in a little Portakabin, so up we used to go once a fortnight, in a place where nobody wanted to go. It was horrific. So of course you were disruptive and you just didn't get on with what you were supposed to have done. And I can't honestly remember what we learnt there. I remember them being quite patronizing, thinking, 'Well, you're all as thick as two short planks.' And you tend to shut off when you're being treated like that. I don't think the tutors were that enthralled by having to come up and deal with us – which I don't suppose *I* would have been, thinking about it.

A generation earlier, Charlie's introduction to the world of work was more basic.

A kettle boy had to make the tea for the men. I used to go up and bring down dynamite to store. Back in they days they stored dynamite anywhere – I had to bring down dynamite from the main magazine, down at Quarry Close. You used to fetch water for the men themselves, then fetch water for the blacksmith and the winderman. You had to do two trips like that, carrying two cans of water, and I'll gamble 'tis nearly quarter of a mile. Then you would have go across the fields and fetch milk from a farmer. When you come back, if there was any trucks being loaded you had to go down and help the clerk to label the trucks. The labels was all written out. You had to go in between the truck and the wharf and put the label in the place, on the other side the truck. By that time you had to come in and get your tea ready for the men.

[There was an] open grate, with a bar going across. Hooks and two great kettles there. You used to have to go out and get wood. The captain wouldn't allow 'ee to have coal, couldn't afford that – go out and pick up wood and burn in that there, and boil the kettles like that. Sometimes the men used to say, 'Tea is some smoky.' What the bloody hell do 'em expect, when you stop and think about it? [We laugh.] 'Twas an old dwelling house. The captain's office was upstairs and the men had the two rooms downstairs for go in have their lunch.

—How old were you when you were a kettle boy?

Fourteen. 'Twas hard work. The men was all right but the captains used to... Everybody was glad to get out of kettle boy. You used to have to carry drills on your shoulder, used to cut in yer. I never forget that, longest day I live. 'Twas slave labour, really. But you wouldn't take no notice of it because everybody used to do it. The men who was kettle boys there, and went in the quarries, done it before you.

Getting There

Before the days of universal car ownership, travel was either an adventure or an endurance test. Bob:

Initially, before he lodged in Bugle and then got married, my great grandfather, my father's grandfather, walked to and from St Columb every day, to Bugle. Five or six, seven miles. 'Tis a fair little jaunt. Henry Hawk was telling me that his grandfather used to live at Lostwithiel and drove the pumping engine at Wheal Cock clay works. He used to start out for home on Saturday lunchtime, walk to Lostwithiel [six or seven miles], have Sunday at home. Sunday evening or late afternoon he would pack up a week's supply of food, walk back to Bugle, ready to start the engine for Monday morning. And then he would live in the engine house, sleep on the settle and tend the engine and stoke the fires, and stay there 24 hours a day until Saturday lunchtime when they shut down.

Pre-war – it's incredible now to think that – I don't think that I'd been anywhere hardly out of Bugle, pre-war. Course, I was a tacker of a schoolboy, but if you went on the Great Western as we called the local bus service, Western National, and went to St Austell, 'twas, oh a marvellous job, 'twas an incredible way away and ages on the bus and cost thruppence, for instance.

When I was at Camborne [School of Mines] I used to bike to and fro weekends. Usually we were up at the mines surveying underground Saturday mornings. And then Saturday afternoon usually I would play hockey, and then come back to the club and have a bath, and put my week's washing and my homework on the back of my bike, and bike Bugle. That's 40 miles, something like

Clarence Hancock, summer 1999.

that. [More like 50, round trip!] And then Sunday, if 'twas rain I'd bike in St Austell and put my bike on the train, and if 'twas dry weather I'd bike Camborne again. Lodge down there during the week.

—That's a fair old bike ride – in Cornwall!

Yeh, but once I got up to Zelah – Zelah was my cut point. I used to think, even if they knock me off my bike they won't bloody eat me now, I'm back in white man's country more or less. [Laughs.] Goss Moor was hard. You see the bridge up at the end of Goss Moor two mile away, and two hours later he's still two miles away and you're pedalling. Goss Moor was a peculiar road. Only road I know is uphill both ways and always head wind, whichever way you'm going.

The Machines

Right up until the middle years of the century, steam-powered beam engines were still extensively used. But whatever the power source, the job of pump-man was special. Bob remembers.

—*I suppose if you lived alongside the steam engine all the time, you could easily detect a change – if something was wrong?*

Oh yes. If they're sleeping and the engine starts to slow or anything untoward happen, they're awake in a minute. 'Tis their job. When centrifugal pumps came in, in the beginning of this [the twentieth] century, and beam engines then were on their way out, the new pits had centrifugal pumps [which] could switch on and off fairly easily, so they wouldn't work more or less continuously. They would shut down when the shift finished – and then spring water would start to pool up in the bottom of the pit, and the pump-man would get in a couple of hours before the shift start, to pump out that water that had accumulated overnight. If it came to a stream of rain, a flash flood, he would have to go in because the pump would be drowned. You might have – on a big old pit – might be say ten acres in there. That'll catch a fair amount of water if you get an inch of rain in an hour, and when you come down to the cone bottom you might find you got 20ft of water there, fairly quickly. The story in the village was, that to be a pump-man you had to be able to sleep with one leg out of the window.

By twenty-first-century standards, it was low technology. This had its advantages. Bob again:

Now when everything is working right, apart from stoking the boiler every two or three hours there isn't a lot to do. But you got to be there in case the engine changes note and – she's gone in fork [run out of water] or picked up a wood chip under the valve, in which case there's something to be done. His job was a 24-hour job, five and a half days a week.

There is a story in Bugle – there was a fair amount of boiler bursts in the old days – a boiler boiled dry, or the engine driver figured that he couldn't pump fast enough so he would tie the safety valve down or put a 56lb weight on it. Eventually everything would go bang, and they'd bury the dead and rebuild the house and start again. The boiler inspector came around to one clay work, and he said to the engine driver, 'You'll have to shut down right away.' He said, 'I can't shut down, mister, we'm pumpin'.' 'Well,' he said, 'you'll have to shut down right away, there's a steam leak. Boiler's leakin'.' So he said, 'Get away, the boiler isn't leakin'. I was in there a few minutes ago.' 'Come with me.' The boiler inspector went in beside the boiler; he said, 'There, listen. Can't you hear that steam escaping?' 'Aw!' the pump-man said, 'that's nothin' mister,' he said. 'I worked in boiler houses where she do hiss like fuzz adders.'[Laughs]. He didn't count that as a leak, that was nothing to write home about. The story then was that you'd get a shovel and go out and find some fresh horse manure, and release the steam, and open the boiler, and shovel a couple of shovelfuls of horse manure in. Now, the horses were fed on oats and a horse – the metabolism is different from a cow, they aren't such an efficient digester, they don't chew their cud or anything – so in their droppings husks and undigested seed come through. The husks in the water would be sucked to the leaks, and staunch them if you was lucky, if they were small leaks. 'Twas practical, do-it-yourself stuff, and if you made a horrible mistake they phoned the undertaker. It was as easy as that. You was either good at your job, or they was hiring a replacement after they rebuilt.

The Steam Engines

Clarence Hancock worked for a while in the engine house at Greensplat. This engine house survived until, quite recently, it was demolished to make way for more clay-working.

[Father] and the man that built this bungalow here were the shaft men for Greensplat and South Greensplat. There was two pits working back in they days. Their job was to look after the pump gear that's down in the ground. You see, there was a big pumping engine, steam engine. When we were boys, me and my brother, we spent time over there with father when he had to go over and see to some sort of repair, while he was the captain. So we had a pretty good training of it. But I could never keep steam up like the proper engine men could. 'Tis a skill, there's no doubt about it.

—*Were those steam engines still working in your time?*

Yes. I drove it for six months. One man that worked over there – this isn't so long ago, since the war that was – he used to live in St Austell. Going down Trenance one day he fell off his push bike, and he was unconscious for three weeks. They didn't know if he'd ever come back any more or

The beam engine, Greensplat. [WMM]

not, but he did eventually. And while he was away sick, I took over the engine, because I was, like I tell 'ee, Jack of all trades and master of none. I took over the engine, with another man who happens to be my uncle – he was living down Carthew, Uncle Arthur. So you can say 'tis a family work, really.

We've jumped the gun a little bit, but anyhow, I tell 'ee about this chap that had the accident. He used to be able to laugh like a pisky before the accident. D'you know, after that accident he didn't laugh any more. He just carried on with his job, civil to everybody and all that, but you couldn't get him to laugh. No. That's what it did to him.

—*When you opened the door of the engine house, what did you see?*

First thing you see is the brickwork that's around the cylinder of the pumping engine. That was a steel liner in there, for the piston to go up and down. So the first thing you see when you go in the engine house was this yer great brick wall around, in a circle. Then outside that would be this settee that the man would sit on – or go to sleep on if needs be. Because they spent hours down there sometimes, especially if you got rainy weather and you got to start pumping water out in the pit before they can start washing. There was usually two of them doing the day shift. One started very early in the morning, and he leaves work about dinner time. The other one carry on till later in the day. You used to meet the tramps down there. The men that used to travel the roads years ago used to find the little places that they could go to in the winter, get in a warm place somewhere. Well, the winder house was a good place for that. Many a bloke would spend his time down in the boiler house.

—*Did you have to turn them out?*

They'd go on their own. They'd say, 'All right, thank you very much for your company, we'll go on now.' That's the way they used to shift about the country. They'm what we call tramps.

Blasting

Explosives were used extensively in the clay-works – and with much less regard to safety than would be the case now.
—*Before blasting, how did you warn the men working in the bottom of the pit?*

They used to have a bell on top of the pit, and they used to ring this bell. Then the quarries right around – four quarries where I was to – they used to blast a certain time, when the bell goes. Latter years there was a great siren fixed up and everybody in the quarries around this area had to blast to that siren. Eleven o'clock in the morning, we'll just say, and then perhaps two o'clock in the afternoon. That siren wouldn't stop sounding until everybody had phoned in and said, 'All clear'.

I'd taken lunch to my father at work – if Mum was making pasties, during school holidays, wrap up a hot pasty in a clean cloth, and I'd get on my bike and I'd take it to dad for his lunch. This wasn't a daily occurrence, but quite frequently. 'Well if you bring the pasty today, son, bring it to such a side of the pit.' Because he knew where he would be working. I got there, and he was just about preparing to blast. I just sat and watched, and you'd see him put two or three sticks of gelignite down the hole. He'd then make up the primer, make the hole in the cartridge of gelignite. The detonator he would take, tap out the sawdust on his thumb, put the fuse in, put it in his

Charging a hole before blasting in the 1950s. Tommy Richards is on the left, with the ramrod, and Will Brenton has the igniter cord. [GVL]

Emptying a sandpit at Goonvean pit in the 1950s. [GVL]

teeth – no crimpers or anything in those days – it was as simple as that. Detonator in and.... So we knew how to do it. We used to occasionally pinch the odd few sticks of gelignite, some detonators and fuse – this was probably late Saturday afternoon or early evening when there was no-one about. There weren't the laws or the regulations that there are today. The key of the magazine would be kept under a stone or under a piece of slate somewhere, so by watching we knew where the key was kept. We didn't break in anywhere. Then off we'd go, out on the Goss Moor to some of the old pools out there, that had been left from some of the dredging operations – and blast fish.

LS

Enterprise

Traditionally, clay workers often had sidelines – a horse or two they could hire out, backed up by a smallholding or small farm which helped feed the family. Bob:

My grandfather left school when he was nine – dame school – and went wheeling sand for tin streamers. There was still a fair amount of streaming tin in the moors around Bugle. Then he went to clay work. His father had a smallholding and did carting for the clay work. He used his farm horse and cart to carry coal and shift bags of clay around. He also hired his horse out for hoisting on a small clay work close by that couldn't afford a winding engine for hoisting. They used the horse for winding, with a horse whim. [The horse would] walk around and pull the skips of sand out of the pit that way. [Grandfather] used to laugh with the boys saying, 'We three boys and myself work clay work, and the best man for earning is the horse. The horse can earn 3s 6d.' The old man was the best earner, he had 2s 9d I believe, so the horse was the best man out of the five of them.

Hard Graft

Conditions down in the pit were rarely cushy, and often grim, especially before the new technology was introduced. Bob again:

'Tis a snip now. When I joined, in the winter you'd see a feller in oilers twiddling a hand-held monitor firing at the face, and when you went up and spoke to him he would slap the front of his oilers, and a shower of thin ice would slide onto the floor, Now that's tough working conditions!

Men used to take off overburden with a pick and shovel. Sometimes the overburden'd be 3ft deep and sometimes it'd be 60ft deep. Usually, it's 20 or 30. One day, father had a piece to be made by the blacksmith, so he went on to the captain and said, 'Here's the drawings. Blacksmith need to make this up to go with other bits and pieces.' 'Oh yeah Ralph, you better go on and discuss it with en.' Father went in and discussed it with blacksmith, and he

Removing overburden: a captain and workers at Bobas pit, Treviscoe. [WMM]

said, 'I can make it for 'ee, Ralph, but that's a lot of work. I tell you what, I'd like to have somebody with me tomorrow, to strike. 'Tis lot of work, one man with a sledge.' Father said, 'All right, I'll have a word with cap'n, and somebody'll be here in the morning to give 'ee hand.' So next day, lunchtime-ish, Father thought, 'Well, I'd better go on and check and see how 'tis going.' He went in, and one of the burden men had been sent in to do the striking with the blacksmith. Father said, 'Hullo, old man, this is a bit of a change for you. What 'ee think of this then?' 'Aw!' he said, 'damme Ralph,' he said, 'this is nearly as hard's workin'!' That was striking for a blacksmith. He considered he had a day off, really. This was the old style. These people were used to work.

Working Clothes

There were no such things as changing rooms or showers. You went to work in your working clothes and you came home in your working clothes, and changed. You provided your own hobnail boots – in fact there was nothing provided. Their clothes were corduroys, flannel shirts, old tweed jackets; they'd buy second-hand clothes simply to wear to work because you couldn't wear out your best suit fast enough to provide for working clothes.

LS

The Women's Contribution

Although there were no women in the pits or dryers – and that has not changed – women became workers in the clay industry willy-nilly.

Mother had to do all the washing. Really, mother was the sheet anchor of the family because her mother died at a very young age, so she had four brothers, her father who was then a widower, all working in the industry – and she had her husband, my dad, and me growing up. She had to do the baking, the cooking, the washing, for all those.

LS

Monitor Operator

Even in the seventies, when Mike Lamprell started work down the pits, conditions were pretty basic
—When did you start in the clay industry?

In 1974. I started in the pit, on the hose first of all and then on the refining plant. Yes, there was six a shift and two fitters and the day captain. That's all that worked there. It was a bit in the wild. It was hard to get there because it was all old sand roads. And if was going to rain, that's where it was going to rain. Back then most of it was outdoors because it was an old-fashioned settling system. Yes, it was very rough when the weather was bad. I mean, you got oilers: you didn't get wet but it was a pain having to get dressed up sometimes. If one of the skips come off the track at two o'clock in the morning when it was raining – they used to come off the rails sometimes – that was fun! Oilskins, wellington boots, gloves. It was a different era.

—Much the same conditions as back in the thirties?

That pit was, yes. They used to have a beam engine to pump out the pit, and that was

Monitor operators, 1950s. [GVL]

going up until 1956 – something like that, '55. Today, with the Health and Safety at Work Act, they couldn't run it the same. For the motors to the dryers, you had a morse-key switch, you just moved it from one brass stud to the next, and it used to spark off...

—Like the old trams!

Very similar. Speed 1, 2, 3 – bang-bang. Very old fashioned.

—When you were working the hose, were you in a shed?

When I started in '74, they just had their first monitor hut. There was four hoses in the pit; this was the only one that was mechanized. The other three were just a hand-held hose with a galvanized porch over it. But the one I started on had two levers, and two hydraulic rams on the hose, so one went up and down and one went side to side. Every now and again you had to move the hose, because you'd cleared an area, and you had to go out then, but when it was actually washing you could stay inside. They used to change round. The guy on the pump used to go in there for hour and a half or two hours, and the guy on the hose used to go on the hose for two hours, and [then] they used to swap over. Otherwise you'd get soaked. You go in the pump-house to dry out. [The hose shed] kept the wind off, that's about all. You manoeuvred it to where the wind wasn't.

A clay-pit in the Wheal Remfry area, summer 1999.

Course, being down in the pit, and being a small pit, there wasn't that much wind. In the big pits, it's colossal. Being so small – ten acres maybe – probably not that – it was contained. The wind used to go across the top. [In the big pits] if it rains they have to turn the hoses off because the catchment area is so big that the rain comes in and floods the pumps if they don't.

You're very isolated, in the dark, in the pit. They have portable lighting which moves around to where you're working. It doesn't really light the place, it just shines on the face where you're washing. You look back, and it's just total darkness. You can't see anything. And you're all dressed up like the Michelin man.

—*Do they supply you with all this protective clothing?*

Yes. You get overalls – lovely orange colour now; they were nice blue ones back then – wellington boots, ordinary boots, either two-piece or one-piece boiler suits, oilers, donkey jackets. They have high visibility jackets now, lovely yellow colour.

—*When it was time for a break, did you have a room to go into?*

Just about, yes. Galvanized, half-moon shed in the bottom of the pit. No running water, no toilets, not in the pit. If you wanted to go to the toilet you had to come out of the pit, up by the office which was on the top by the refining plant; about quarter of a mile, half a mile. If you wanted water, you had to take the kettle and go down the lane to a spring and fill the kettle up with the spring.

Shift Work

Some men found the isolation of hose-work difficult to endure – that, and the disorientating affect of shift work.

When I used to finish night shift, I couldn't sleep when I came home. The problem is, with the shift work, especially when you're in isolated situations, on the hose or the pump for a long period of time, you didn't communicate. You didn't talk. And that affects you, in respects, when you come home you don't communicate, you don't talk. You become very quiet, very into yourself. You get into a situation where you think a great deal and its not healthy to be thinking in that depth. What happens is, you have a little problem when you go into work, and this will grow into a mountain by the time you came out. Because you had all this time in isolation. They put you in isolation in prison for punishment. We're actually getting paid for this, but it's the same principle. You're in a grey, dank, damp quarry. Half the time the fog was that thick you couldn't see where the bloody hose was, talk about what clay you were washing, so you're just looking at a blanket of nothing. All you could hear is 'sssssssssss' – just this hose. And sometimes you couldn't see what you was washing, you could just hear that you were doing it. Absolute lunacy. And there you are, sitting there. The most you've got to do is push two levers. And it used to drive me round the twist. It used to drive me to despair at times. And you used to look at your watch, you think, 'Oh my god, I've only done an hour. I've got another seven bloody hours of this.' And no communication. And to me that's the worst thing that can happen.

The tough pit life was lightened by the 'characters', usually older workers who had spent a lifetime in the clay.

Most people brought in the pasties. Number of times I've gone into the oven and I've taken the wrong pasty out and I'd started eating it, and some old boy'll come in... "Ere, you got my pasty!' You might just as well have run off with his daughter, eating his pasty. And he'd take my pasty out. He said, 'You got the wrong bloody pasty, you sod.' And there'd be hell, there'd be swearing and all sorts going on over this pasty, and you never done it on purpose – well, perhaps once or twice you would, just to wind him up. And you'd only have a little stub left, just a crust and a little bit of meat. But he'd take this pasty – what you had left – off you, and give you back yours. He wouldn't touch your pasty..... 'Because that'll make me so bad as you, you bloody thief.' And he'd eat the remains of his pasty, so you'd end up having a pasty and three-quarters.

CR

A Different Work Ethic

These older workers observed a different work ethic, based on trust and close personal contact. This was particularly so with the pump-men, who had to get to work early to pump out the pit bottom so their workmates on the hoses could start on time. Clarence Hancock:

Very often we set our alarms so that we got out of bed early enough. We always tried to play it on the safe side. You could tell pretty well what the weather's like when you go to bed. If there was real floods, they may come round and call us all in earlier to get the water out, but most often it was left to

Workers at Greensplat. Clarence's father is on the left.

The engine house at Greensplat in summer 1999. It was demolished a few months later.

the beam-engine man and the other sump men.

—*They must have trusted you.*

They had to, didn'em? They had to, yeah. There was one chap we used to have, driving the Lister engine, driving that gravel pump, and he used to love dance band work. He used to come home from dance band and because of that, if he went home he knowed he wouldn't wake up early enough in the morning for go down sump and pump out, so he used to spend the night in with the beam-engine man. And then he would get woke up by the beam-engine man saying, 'Hey, come on, time for 'ee to go down pit, boy.' Poor old chap, he tried all sorts of things, home, for to wake himself up. He had two baths once, and he put alarm clocks in the baths hoping they'd rattle more. Because he used to go dead to the world when he went to sleep.

I don't think 'tis worked on the same basis that we used to work. Not with the same feeling of urgency, that this is my job, and I must look after en.

Clay-Dries

Work in the clay-dries was hot, sweaty and almost completely manual. Les Lean remembers:

I worked in Wheal Martin dry myself, where the museum is now. No electric lights in there then. You go up in the morning, light the lantern, carry the lantern in there, change. First of all you'd throw off what's on the pan. All the clay what you bring in one day would be dry overnight from when you left it, say from one dinner time to next morning. We used to start about five o clock and take most of the clay off the pan, in over – in the linhay it was called – down under. And then go out with the wagons, bring it in, more muck stuff. You go in there on a hot pan, sweating, then you'd be outside in all... it was raining – winter time – go out there and shovel it in, and get drowned and cold. When you finish up, you always go home with the same white... you see everybody's white, going home. Old men always be white, up in the clay dust, no showers or nothing like that, for to wash off. My granddad worked in a dry like that, and he used to go home – that's Wheal Martin – and he used to come home up Hensbarrow, up through Carthew, cut up through the moor and up through his place, and uncle said he had a hessian sack round his shoulders. He'd take hessian sack off, come inside, stand in front the Cornish range, his back towards the Cornish range, and the steam would be flying from him. He wouldn't change.

I was down Charlestown clay dry at the time – and it was great, lovely. Then we had a manager come there, and he wanted to save coal so he made this great big metal door with a little four inch hole in it, and in the night he would close this big door down the back [of

A clay-dry at Wheal Martyn. [WMM]

In Blackpool pit. The worker on the left is holding a dubber. [RCM]

the flues] and just have this small hole. Cor! You go in in the mornings there, you could feel the heat before you go up in the dry. Red hot. You was there shovelling off the front, what we call the fore end, up near the fires, shovelling off there and, oh, it'd nearly kill you, man. We used to have wood clogs for on the pan, yeah. We had to change they, two or three times, before you go across the pan, 'tis so hot. So when I seen something, to get out of it, I done it.

After working in the clay dry, Les became a coalman.
—But coal work must have been pretty strenuous?

Yeah, but that wasn't nothing like in the clay dry. People say to me, 'Cor, how d'you...?' I say, 'My dear, that isn't a patch on in the clay dry.' The heat was so unbearable we were stripped to the waist all the year round, winter or nothing, stripped to the waist all the time.

—Shovelling all the time?

Yes. Seen those big shovels? I expect the pan was about 18ft wide. In the clay-dry we used to go across – vroom! – and pull it back and tip it over the wall.

—You didn't put on a lot of weight then!

Missus'll say I was like a whippet [he laughs]. I was. I got so bad that I used to wake up in the night jumping, keyed up like. Because you had to get up here, four o'clock in the mornings. You couldn't sleep right, thinking about it before you get there.

Dressing Up

Before very high-pressure hoses were in use, there were sometimes two teams of men, one on the top of the pit cliff-face, one on the pit floor, both washing down the clay. It was muddy work, and 'special' clothing was worn! George Morcom:

Back at that time you had a stream coming down over the side of the pit, coming down over the clay, and the men would be up there, maybe four or five up there, digging into that stream. The stream would be washing down, and the hose would be smashing it up when it gets to the bottom. It was nothing to see four men up there breaking in the strake – they call that a strake, the water coming down. These dubbers the blacksmith made on the clay-works, they were like a one-pointed pick, and it would have a piece set back over the back to strengthen it so that when the pick was down, they could lift up for to prize it out, these lumps. The water'd be going down and you'd make a gully, hacking into the gully. That would gradually come down over the pit, and the hose down the bottom would be washing up as well.

—So you'd have some blokes at the top of the pit by the stream, and some blokes down the bottom on the hose, all washing clay out?

All washing the same amount of clay, yeah. And that hadn't changed for years. Then it got that they had more pressure on the hoses, they done away with these men up in the strake.

—Sounds like a pretty mucky job.

Yes. You had rubber boots on. When I went there first, there was another man took on in the morning – I was the afternoon shift. He took the boots off, and I put them on. So they didn't have a chance to dry, did they! By this time we had rubber boots – leather bottoms, hobnails in them. We used to use a piece of hessian, wrap your foot in the hessian with your stocking on, and when you take it off in the evening that hessian would be streaming wet with sweat – but your wool sock would still be dry. Then you'd hang it up for the next day. It'd be smelling quite high in that place, in the boot house.

Previously to that they used to use leather boots which they used to call washers' boots, leather up to the knee. The local cobblers used to make them. The leather would be bought from Crockens's tannery at Probus. They made most of their leather with bark from oak trees. There's woods over there, used to be known as Queen's Wood and Bishop's Wood. [The oak bark] would be taken over to Probus to make the tannic acid to tan the leather. About 1960-odd we were digging there in an old place in the pit where there was an old level, and we found a pair of boots there that may have been there for twenty years. I took them up to a bloke called Whitrose Vear. He cleaned them up and re-stitched them, and you'll find them out Wheal Martyn, in the museum.

The local cobbler's shop was really a area where the blokes would come in the evenings, because the cobbler'd be working on late. He'd made a part of the boot, we'll say the leg part, and he would stitch it, and to make it more watertight he would turn it inside and out like you turn a stocking inside and out. But that's really stiff leather, wasn't it. Took a bit of doing, didn't it.

Rostowrack stone quarry, 1950s. The steep-sided quarry walls are quite different from those in clay quarries. [GVL]

There'd be four or five chaps from the village there – in fact I've been there myself, because my granfer used to live close by. I've gone over once or twice – only a candle in there to see by. He had these local boys around there and he would say, 'Yer, turn that one inside out for me; I'll give you two bob.' Well, they'd be trying and trying and trying, and he'd be keeping an eye on them, because all the time they're making it more pliant. After a time he would say, 'Yer, give en to me; I'll show you how to do it.' He would put his hand down through and pull it up yer, see. He wouldn't give nobody two bob.

Around the down there was a grass that used to dry up there, the winter time. The old men would pick that and take it home in a bag, and bring some each week with them to shove down in the bottom of the boot. And also stick pieces down the other way to tighten up the boot so there wasn't much slack in it. They were really heavy boots to wear. But they wasn't moving around a lot with 'em, they'd be standing at one place.

Roped Up

Charlie worked in a clay-stone quarry. These lumps of rock had to be pulverized before use. The method of obtaining the material was quite different from the hose system used in the clay-pits, and was more like normal stone quarrying. But leg-pulling was as much part of the working life in the quarries as it was in the pits.

We used to go down on the sides of the quarry on ropes. Used to tie a rope round yourself, on top of the quarry, used to bore down a hole and put an iron bar down in there. Then you would tie your rope to the iron bar and lower yourself down on the sides of the quarry until you get to the place where you want to go.

—Sounds dangerous.

It may seem dangerous to people who never done it, but to we people, we never took no notice of it at all. Take no more notice of going down on the sides of a quarry, 100ft down the side of a quarry – you didn't take no notice of it. But nowadays people call that dangerous. Back in those days you was brought up to it. Its exactly the same as a boy learning tennis. He starts off with hitting the ball around. Well, you would start off down the bottom of the quarry. You gradually say, 'Oh well, I'll go up there and do that there.' It comes to 'ee naturally. Some people couldn't do it, mind you. 'Tisn't everybody have got the nerve.

Always tie the rope round *yourself*. Never trust nobody else. A bowline. Won't slip. Years before I finished, they brought out the leather belts with the buckle. You slide your rope through the buckle and tie it. But when I started there was no such thing as leather belts. You just tied the rope round yourself; a manila rope round yourself, tie the knot and go down over. If you was going down over a vertical face you would go down with your feet stuck into the face of the quarry, and with a rope. You would walk down over the side of the face.

—You need strong arms and legs.

You wouldn't be in there if you never had strength, because 'twas hard work. Quarry work was hard work. You never see very many weaklings in the quarry. I've been down over the sides of a.... I've been down the ladders of a quarry, down 130ft, with the ladder staves covered with ice. You would go

Will Brenton is drilling popping holes – for splitting the stone blocks with dynamite – at Rostowrack quarry in the 1950s. [GVL]

down and do the best you can. You would never give in. You'd go down in the mornings at seven o'clock, and you'd come up to have crib [clay-workers' name for a meal break] half past nine. You have your food, and then you go down again ten o'clock. Come up again twelve o clock.

—That's a lot of climbing up vertical ladders!

Nine times out of ten, if somebody was going up there, somebody was telling a bloody tale and they'd stop, talking, and you would stop – this is how it used to be like. If we thought we was too early go up, you put the slowest man up in front [laughs]. Oh, used to see some carry on. Fun! 'Twas a pleasure to go work. I know

you had to work hard but 'twas a pleasure to go work for the fun you used to have. Joking, leg pulling. 'Twas endless, 'twas endless.

The poor old captain use to be religious, see, and every crib [break] time, after twenty minutes was up – he would be sitting down with 'ee, mind you – and his watch would come out like this yer, see. Time was up. You knew, like. And there was a chap sitting right opposite en, and the times he would say, 'We had some good service up Carne Hill last night!' Old captain used to say, 'Who was there?' – and 'twas nothing more to hang on another five, ten minutes every crib time.

—Are any of the china stone quarries still working?

No. No quarry working, not now. The only quarries working is at Rostowrack and at the moment all they'm doing there is crushing stone for building materials and filling. That's the place where I used to be a captain, but I haven't been in there, not since I finished work.

—*Could those pits be re-opened?*

No. They're all filled in now. All filled in bar one, and that's being used for a water reservoir, for cleaning lorries.

New Machines

John Cloke drives large earth-moving vehicles. His enthusiasm for these machines matches that of the older workers for their beam engines.
—*What's this new truck that you're driving now?*

The new CAT 950G. It's a rubber-tyred front-end loader. I remove the stent from the face so as you can wash the clay. I remove the rock. They turn the monitor away from you, then you go in and pick it up. You just make big heaps of waste rock – you just tip it up in a big heap in the bottom of the pit and then the dump trucks will come in and remove it. We've got airsprung seats, so you adjust your seat to your weight. You ride with the machine. It's a lot better than the previous model was.

—*What are the improvements?*

Visibility, driver comfort, the controls – its all electronic, computerized. Whereas before it would be manual gear change, or semi-automatic gear change. The easier 'tis, the faster 'tis, the quicker you can work. It's easier than driving a car. Everything is worked by oil, air or electric. My bucket controls [are] about inch and a half long. All worked by electric. It's so easy, you don't even know you're working any more. Just finger-tip controls. There's

A front-end loader at work.

Inside the cab of a front-end loader.

a load computer. It weighs how much you pick up in your bucket, your bucket cycles, your stop time; tells you how much you've done per shift. Record it. Then they come out with a laptop computer, download that, take it back to our main depot and put it into the main computer. That way they know how long you stopped, how long you worked, how much you've done. Spy in the cab. They can put one man against another: 'He's done 500 ton per shift, you've done 300 ton per shift. Why haven't you done as much as he?' It records everything that engine does. Every rev.

His job has its own special risks.

You've got the hose-man, but you're not working in close proximity with any other machine. You're always working on your own, and that's what I like as well. You aren't looking out for somebody else. Yes, you've got to watch the hose-man, you've

got to watch he put the hose out of your way. He's got to watch you. You've got to have trust in each other. I've got to trust that hose-man because if he make a mistake he can kill me, the same as if I reverse back and turn too quick, I can kill he. With that hose, it's coming out, I think, 1,500psi. He'll go right through a cab and he will take a person's head off, easy. And when it comes out that nozzle it's like a steel bar. If you could see what that hose will do to metal sometimes, you haven't got much hope against glass and flesh. And you'm working within five, six feet of that. If that can tear stone out the ground, and tear clay out the ground, and cut holes in a clay face, a human being haven't got much chance against it.

We got one hose-man in particular who, the minute you engage reverse gear, he's got his hose coming back on 'ee. The minute you engage gear – you still haven't moved and he's still got that hose coming back onto your machine. They smash our cab glass out scores of times. Stones through the cab. You got this pressure of the hose hitting the face; everything's flying away, so the small stones fly like bullets. It is safety glass, so within reason you've got a brave protection between you and the stones. But they do come through the cab and out the other side. I've been in the cab several times and ended up with stones in my lap, the glass completely gone and the cab full of glass and sand.

—*And in the old machines? What were they like?*

Heater, if you was lucky, and if 'twas hot you put your windows down and you got buried in dust. You had water-carts trying to keep your dust down. You come home and you'd be covered in dust. Straight in the bath. Now, to get the best out of air conditioning, you close your windows. You got re-circulated air, you got fresh air. You'm cool all the time. Lovely. We got radio cassettes built into the cab. You got music all day long. In our excavators we've got two way radio communication with the management, with our depot, with the fitters – but that is to give you orders. You've got stereo radio cassette all built in. Its home from home. You spend more hours a day in your machine at work than what you do your car.

The driver's view of the pit face and monitors at work.

CHAPTER 3

Work Outside the Clay-works

A Cornish hedge at Gunheath Hill.

Building Hedges

The mid-Cornish man-made landscape has three main features: enormous craters, huge spoil mounds – and Cornish hedges. These are found everywhere in the county, and Les Lean's father used to build them.

Father was born down Perranporth, then he came – when he was fourteen, that's 1904 – came up Old Pound. [He built] hedges all round Karslake. There's still one going up Gunheath Hill, going from Carthew, on the right-hand side.

—I suppose you can't easily destroy one of those hedges.

They've tried. ECLP have taken out several chunks for different things – for a pump-house. That was [father's] full time job. He worked for the council then, on building hedges. I've seen them being built – but not so long ago as that. Yes, built them myself. They have a wood frame up, the same shape. Had a bit of string going across to know the same shape to go up. You dig down in the ground a little bit, dig a wide trench about 4ft [wide] I suppose, about a foot or so below the ground. And then you start off the bottom ones, bigger stones in the bottom. They gradually go up straight and the last row would be stood up straight. Then they filled it up with earth inside, tamping it down, and then put turf on the top – or tabs, we used to call it.

—So you have a stone wall on two sides?

That's right. And fill up the middle with earth.

—Did he build walls where the rows were zig-zag?

Oh no. That was a smaller stone. You get them on the north coast, more. More slaty stones. There's a modern one up near the viaduct, only built two or three years ago, so someone's doing it now.

—Where did they get the stone from?

From the downs, then. Pick up stones, find stones. 'Twas better stone than 'tis now, more natural. All the stone now come from quarries, but the old hedges, they were natural stone. Different colour, different kind of stone altogether. Years ago, up our way, they used to leave a hole in the bottom of a hedge. I don't know if for pigs going through or back along a lot of geese were going through. 'Tis a nice job. Fresh air, in the rain.... My mother talked about people that used to be up – she had a lodger once who used to be up

A Cornish hedge – end-on view.

A Cornish hedge – the north coast version. This one is in the Gover valley, St Austell.

breaking stone for the roads. Used to employ stone breakers on the side of the road, breaking stone all day long. That was a wearisome old job. When you're building a hedge you can see some of your labour. Look back on, and pass by and see a nice bit of workmanship. But just breaking up stone, that's tiresome, I should have thought. No end product.

—Do they plant those bushes you see on the top?

No. Just grow there. As a matter of fact, that destroys a lot of the hedges because the roots'll go down and throw the stone out. There's some nice hedges around. If you go from Market House [St Austell] up through to North Street there's a nice hedge on the side going up there. Very

narrow road, as you leave the town and just go up that hill. You seen that stone hedge there? Lovely one. Oh lovely. And sometimes, where the bushes are, they've thrown some of the stone out now, pushing them out.

Trains

When Colin Croker was young, the St Blazey/Par area was a busy rail centre for both passenger and freight (mostly clay) traffic.

I was [a trainspotter] as a young boy in the forties and fifties. Everything was steam, and mostly they were the mineral tankies. They didn't have a big tender behind. They were mostly 45s, 55 class, and the tankies, those were the little – I think

48

they had six wheels, three driving and that was it – and they were mostly shunting. An old 45 would – I've seen 'em struggling – and they would pull say thirty to forty 13-ton trucks, so they were good work-horses. But they used to double them up, put bankers on. They'd have one engine in the front and one at the back, one would be pushing and one would be pulling, I've heard the driver say that it was considered good driving if they could get the middle link slack. If there was say, thirty trucks on, and the fifteenth truck – the actual chain link between 'em was slack – it meant that the front engine was pulling and the back engine was pushing an equal amount.

GWRs always had a different look. God's Wonderful Railway – it was considered the best of all four railways. They were the safest. I'll give you an instance, down at Par, if you went from Par to Fowey with a trainload of clay, when you went through the level crossing at Par they had a key, which the driver would give to the signalman to unlock the next link. Nobody could go on that link until the key was handed back. So you would get this situation where they'd be belting up the track, leaning out to pass this key or collect it. If they missed it, they had to stop the train and go back and fetch it. All done on the move.

—*How many people would be working a train like that? You have a driver and…*

…A fireman. And then on the brake-van at the very back – and GWRs were peculiar in shape because they had a little roof, a place about 10, 15ft by about 8ft, a little cabin – and then they had a little veranda out over. That was where the brake was, so [the brakeman] could be out there and he could view everything from the back. He was a pretty key man. I've got it in remembrance of one in particular – I was working for a builder at the time, and we were down at Par. One of these trains went out across Par beach into Fowey through the tunnel, with a load of clay trucks on. We seen him go across the beach, up through, and about ten minutes later we could hear this whistle blowing. Looked down beach and there was a train coming back down, the same train, with the guard's van in front now, going quite fast. The guard was in there blowing his whistle but there was no engine on the end. The coupling had broke, up in the tunnel. Course, its hell of a steep incline. Eventually it had come to a stop, the train had. Engine went on, and he ran back. The guard stayed with his train and he wound everything on that he could, but there were several hundred tons – get a big incline like that – the train just ran on right across the beach, which is nearly a mile, under the five arches and back towards the level crossing he'd gone over. He was blowing his whistle and the signalman opened all the points, and he came right through the sheds onto this embankment before he stopped. The funny thing was, about three minutes later the engine come belting back, whistling and blowing – 'Anybody seen my train?' – it was comical and yet it would have been lethal if they hadn't cleared the line right through. [The signalman] didn't have a chance to open the level crossing gates, and they just went through like matchwood. A coach full of holidaymakers from Newquay missed it by a few feet. That would have been on the level crossing a few seconds earlier.

English China Clays Shipping Department office, St Austell, c. 1924. [RCM]

Offices

John Hooper worked in one of the clay company offices in the forties, using what seems like a nineteenth-century method of copying correspondence.

Although typewriters were in use in the office, they still didn't use carbon papers and copies [but] the old method of the copybooks, which were tissue papers. They were in a very heavily bound book of a thousand sheets of tissue, and they were all numbered. Quarto size. Letters and invoices each day were typed with a different type of ribbon. It was a more or less indelible ink. You went through the procedure of first laying on the last tissue that had been used a piece of waterproof card. That protected the last letter that was in there. You had a damp cloth, you put that on top of the protective card. Then you turned over a new tissue, the next blank tissue, onto the damp [cloth]. You had the letter or invoice, and you laid that face down on the tissue. After that there was another piece of damp material laid on the back of the letter, followed by another waterproof on the back of that. You might have one letter to do – I think you could perhaps do two or three at a time. You gradually built it up, and then you closed the book, put it in a big metal press and you'd wind it down. It would remain in there for a short while, maybe half an hour, after which you'd unwind the press and go through the procedure of taking out everything that you'd put in. The indelible ink from the letter or invoice would come off onto the tissue paper.

Whatever number the tissue was, you then entered that number against the surname or title of the company that you'd written the letter or sent the invoice to. Wonderful system, but very time-consuming. When you'd taken the letters out, you had to peg them onto a little line to thoroughly dry. After they were dry they'd be taken down, folded up and put into their envelopes. And the usual procedure of entering them in the postage book at whatever rate they were being sent, at whatever weight they might be. You had office scales there. If you thought they were going to be over and above a certain weight, then the extra postage would have to go on, and that would be entered in the book as well.

We didn't have any biro pens then. Little porcelain ink pot – sometimes they were ornate glass ones, sometimes glass or porcelain ones, within a wooden surround.

And an ordinary pen. No we weren't back to the quill, not quite so far back as that. [He chuckles.]

Shipping

After the war John Hooper's work became more interesting, perhaps, but more responsible.

I had the chartering of the vessels from local ship brokers – there were three or four ship brokers in the area. You had the job of going down to Charlestown, after the shipbrokers informed you of the arrival of the vessel in the dock – you'd have to go down there and climb down into the hold, with vertical ladders. I didn't like it at first.... You get used to it, and it was your job to inspect the hold. If you'd chartered the vessel it was for you to decide if the hold was clean enough to accept a bulk cargo. It's not like having a

Mevagissey harbour, summer 2000.

The outer harbour wall at Mevagissey, summer 2000.

product in packaging. It was a loose bulk cargo that came down the chutes into the vessel. Sometimes the vessels would come into Charlestown with cargoes of cement or coal, and they would have to be washed out.

Fishing

Most Mevagissey folk still depended for fishing for their livelihoods when Caroline Smale was a young woman.

There was the fish factory in Mevagissey, on Tregony Hill, where they used to kipper the herrings, and my mum did work some time there during the winter, to help out. A lot of Scotch girls used to come to do the kippering, from Aberdeen, Shetland Isles. We had a spare room in our house and we used to have five, I think it was, lodge with us most of the winter. They had two rooms in our house, one turned into a living room. All five would sleep in one room. It was a cottage-type house, but the rooms were fairly big. They'd arrive with their big wooden trunks full of clothes and they'd use those, with cushions on, for their seating. It was an old-fashioned cottage with, in the bedroom, open fire grates, so they had a lovely fire. They'd be as happy as anything up in their rooms, knitting their Fair Isle jumpers. We had beautiful Fair Isle jumpers and caps, my sister and I. Four of them came to us for about seven or eight years. For years and years and years we corresponded with them, until they passed away. From Lerwick and Stornoway ours were, from the Shetland Isles. A lot of houses in Mevagissey had them.

CHAPTER 4

Patronage, Bosses and Workers

Mr Varcoe's pit, Greensplat, summer 1999. The old engine house is in the background.

Mr Varcoe

After the Second World War, many of the *minor clay companies were amalgamated into English China Clays (ECC). But the old style of personal employer/employee relations persisted. Workers knew their bosses (such as R.J. Varcoe, see below) by name, and the company took an interest in the villages and the village people. This personal approach gradually became eroded.*

—*Did you know Varcoe?*

Oh yes. Used to see him quite often. First going off when we met him, was when he had that big house, the Arts Theatre, and he wanted turf for a lawn, so he gave my father a job in the evenings to go over there, in that there loop in the road, over there, South Greensplat, and cut out the turf. Then Giles's family, that had team of horses, they used to come here then next day, pick up the turf, carry it into St Austell. The next evening father'd be over cutting more. Well quite often Mr Varcoe would come up and see what the turf was like before we start cutting, so we've met en pretty often.

—*At least you knew your boss in those days.*

Yes, you could talk to en, and all that. You don't know who is the real bosses now, do 'ee? But with all these men, it depends on how you talk to them. You mustn't know too much. You must leave they to know, mustn't 'ee.

CH

Hanging Church Bells

The company, years ago, used to do a lot in the the villages, when they had quite a big engineering force. If church bells needed to be re-hung, the company would do that. One or two of the villages have got playing fields. The company would give them the land, and they'd send a bulldozer out there for a week to level it. Now, there isn't the engineering workforce there used to be, because a lot of it now contracted out, so the whole nature of the thing is changing.

LS

Pensioners' Lunch

[ECC] used to provide a pasty lunch for the pensioners once a year. All the pensioners used to go up to John Keay House, they had a big marquee out the back. They only had a pasty and a cup of tea, but they used to see all the people they used to work with, and

they all loved it. It cost about £1,000 a year, and they stopped it to save money. In the scale of things, £1,000 is absolutely nothing to ECC. One of our big valves is £1,000, so it's penny-pinching. But it's damaged their public relations. It's all trivial little things, I know, but it adds up.

ML

Cradle to the Grave

It was a very similar thing to how they used to work in the coal mines. If you worked for the company, they provide you with a house, provide you with a job – and then during the sixties and seventies they had this fantastic welfare department to look after their employees. It was on the philosophy, from the cradle to the grave. They would nurture and care for you, to an extent, right the way through.

CR

Old-Style Bosses

If you had a problem, you saw your works captain. He would know you, he would know your father, he would know your history. If 'twas financial problems you was in, you see your manager. He would sort things out with John Keay House, whether 'twas your rents or mortgage, or you was behind with your debts. ECLP would take the money out of your wages to make sure 'twas paid. When I had my first mortgage, back in 74/75, my mortgage was arranged by Mr Prior, my works manager. I never had to have no medicals. I never had no references. We just had to go in and sign the papers.

That was how ECLP run. They would bend over backwards to make sure their employees was OK.

JC

Changes

Bob's father saw the approaching changes in management style.

When I came home [from Canada] I said I was going to enquire off the clay company – about the only time that I have ever not taken [my father's] advice – he never gave advice in the normal sense but we'd chat, and you'd get the idea. He said, 'Well I dunno boy, you do what you like; I shall be glad see you home here. But there's a new crowd in charge of the clay company – they'll bring rags to our arse before they finish.' I said, 'How do 'ee think that?' 'Well,' he said, 'they'm spending somebody else's money.' Up until now all the directors had been people that had grown up in the clay industry, and had their own money, and probably borrowed money as well, in it. There was the Nicholses and Selleck and Frank Parkyn and all these people that – they owned their works as well as being managing director of two or three pits. 'Twas theirs. There was other shareholders, but they were *the* principal, or a principal, shareholder. [Father] said, 'When you'm spending your own money you'm in a different class from raising shareholders' money and spending it. You shouldn't be, but you are.'

A generation later, and the signs were more manifest…

They used to keep their lorries clean. They looked beautiful – blue, with ECC sign on the side, always spotless. Now they don't. The reason they don't is because the customers say, 'If it's costing you twenty-five quid to clean that lorry, leave it dirty and charge twenty-five quid less.' Its not ECC's fault, but 'tis what people see, the community see. The rail wagons, they were all emblazoned with 'ECC International' on the side, and the pit sign in blue; the stainless steel containers used to shine, like…. Now they're not cleaned, they're filthy. Terrible. That's the way ECC have gone, and its hard – harder for others than me because I only caught the end of the goodies. But those that have worked there since the early sixties – and there's still some there, it's a different company completely. The morale of the workforce is going down all the time.

ML

Too Impersonal

There is no doubt that many workers resent the new, impersonal management style, especially when a long line of family connection to the clay industry is broken. John Cloke:

My granfer Newland, Mum's father, worked at Halviggan pit. My father worked for ECLP, my uncles worked for ECLP, my brother worked for ECLP till they laid en off through his disability. I work for ECLP. It was father to son, father to son. I tried to get my son into the firm, which he wanted, being a local person, and they didn't want to know. He applied, and I was told by John Keay House, It's better for your boy to look for work elsewhere rather than look for

ECLP, because we won't take him on. They used to employ between 10,000 and 12,000 men when I started. They'm down to about 3,000 men now.

The aspect of the industry has changed dramatically since I started in August of '67. It's gone from a family-run concern, where you were a name, to where you're just a works number now. You prided yourself. You was part of a family. Everybody respected you. You was proud to say you was associated with ECLP. The managers were all local men, they worked their way up from kettle boy, up through the system. They did the same thing as you did. You were happy to go to work. You had fun at work. I go to work now to bring a wage home for my wife, daughter and myself. I go to work, I switch my brain off, and I keep watching my watch until it's time to leave work. I come back, I change my boots and I switch my brain back on. There's no morale left. All 'tis, is push push push push.

John's attitude to working for the new, multinational organization contrasts strongly with the commitment of earlier generations. His view of the future is bleak.

I go what they call second crib break. When that man comes out, I go in. Sometimes I'll go in a bit early, if I want to see the other drivers to discuss something – but if I go in early I come out early. If you go crib, and you'm having laugh and joke with your other workmates, it give you incentive to be there. But when you go crib and you'm on your own – night shift, one o'clock in the morning and you go to have crib in a little crib hut on your own – you don't want to stay there. You feel that you want to get out and do a bit extra. But you think, 'Sod 'em, why should I?' So you have a few minutes

longer. They've taken away all our incentive to work, they've taken away our initiative to be happy. There's no more laughing and joking.

They aren't taking no younger ones on. There isn't many younger than me, driving. As men retire, their jobs aren't being taken. When I started, back in 1967, if fifty men retired fifty men was taken on, younger. So as sixty-five-year-olds was retiring, twenty-five-year-olds were starting. You had a continuous supply. There was no age gaps. There's only one reason I can see they've done this – the generation that come on after me is the last one. Close ECLP down. ECLP is finished.

Take-over

John Hooper's family firm was one of those taken over during the years of amalgamation. It was not a painless experience.

Yes, that came in 1965, I think it was. It was a bolt out of the blue. It was unfortunate really. Our little company, we were only one of dozens of small companies that was controlled by a big investment company within the City. It just happened that one day the big white chief came in and decided that – picked out dozen or more names – Sell them off. We just happened to be one of them, and that was that.

—*So you were actually sold to ECLP?*

Yes, as I understand it.... There's no way that you can compete with such a big concern. You relied on them to assist in many ways. At the time I was extremely upset at what had happened. Whatever it was that brought it about was no fault of ECLP. They may have felt obliged to take on everybody that was employed by the old company – which they did. Every man Jack that worked in our company had a job with ECC, but of course it wasn't quite the same as what you had before.

It was common for Cornishmen with mining experience to spend some time working abroad. Bob's father, and later Bob himself, both did this, and then returned to the clay country. This transfer was made easier because both men knew the clay bosses well.

Father went to Africa before he was married, so he came home with a big pile of money – that's what he bloody went for! When he came back, because he'd been well known in the clay-works, as a young man, from being a good engineer and installing bits and pieces – when he came back on his leave from his second contract he happened to meet a chap in the road, and this chap said, 'Didn't know you was home, Ralph. I got a job for you.' 'Oh well, I'm on holiday....' 'Yeh, but look, I'm stuck a bit. I wonder if you can come up and give us a hand....' Then, while he was doing that, before he'd finished, Claud Selleck come and said, 'Christ, I didn't know Ralph was working for you.' 'Well I ain't working for anybody for a minute, hang on!' Selleck said, 'I want another gas engine put in. I wonder....' 'Well,' he said, 'I can't do it anyway, Claud; a) I'm on holiday and b) I'm working for Willy.' 'Oh, I got a man that'll do Willy's job, you come and work for....'

So he swapped over. He never did join Selleck. He was never hired. Selleck always had another job to be done, and then when Selleck got taken over, Selleck stipulated that two or three of his key men should have a job as long as they wanted one, so father

had a job guaranteed for life. That was Selleck's style. Selleck used to have a saying to all his men. I give you buggers hell, but don't you ever forget, I never let anybody else do it, do I? Now when he became a director of the combine, if any of the other bosses interfered with any of his men the smoke would fly. 'You tell me. I'll decide who's going to have hell and who isn't. Don't you interfere with my men. They'm my men.'

When, after his own spell abroad, Bob returned to Cornwall and took up a supervisory position in the clay industry, he continued the informal approach to the men in his charge.

My contract men used to make me laugh – afterwards. Make me sweat at the time. When things was going good in the old pan kiln, I can go in the morning, just walk through, that's all. If they speak, you got a problem, and you deal with it. If you haven't, you've shown the flag – walk in one end, out the other, they've had their chance. If things was going good they say, 'Hullo Bob, picking beans yet, or digging tatties?' I was Bob, and we was mates together. Another morning they say, 'We been waiting for you, Mr Bugger. Have a look at this.' The coal would be from the wrong colliery and the flame wouldn't be long enough, or the muck in the tank would be stiff, or shovel handles would be breaking because they'd bought cheap bloody park-shovel handles. I was promoted to Mr Bugger those days. I used to think, 'I'm going to earn [my wife's] pasties for her today, that's for certain,' because it could get hot here in a minute. Because the feller that's prepared to fight a contract and make big money, is also prepared to fight the manager. He's the sort of man you want; you ain't looking for a pussy cat. You'm looking for a man tiger to start with, and when he's in step with you, you got a bloody good mate, and when he's fierce and going to scratch your eyes out, you got a fight on.

Work Rhythms

Farmworkers sometimes transferred to the clay industry – but the work rhythms on the land and those in the clay industry were quite different. Bob:

Captain come to me, he said, 'There's a chap, a farmer's given up, he's looking for a job, and his next door neighbour – who was a bloody good workman – wondered if he could work here, because they could ride to and fro in the same car.' I said, 'Right, tell him he can start. I'm a man short anyway. He got the right background; two weeks' trial, if that suit en.' So he come and we put him to wash out trucks for filling. Truck might have had anything in, might even have had coal in it, or sometimes British Rail trucks was rotten in the bottom, and you had to wash that out because it had to be clean. We put him with a gantry and a hose, washing out trucks. The shunt would go through slowly, with the back truck door open, a tipping truck, and he would wash them out. He'd been working there several days for us, maybe a week, sweeping up and cutting ditches and washing trucks. He wasn't bloody lively. I saw him and I said, 'Now look, boy, 'tisn't going to work out; week's notice.' He said, 'Oh, well, I don't know what I'm doing wrong. I'm working like I always work.' I said, 'Perhaps so. You been farm labourer, and you know that you got ten or twelve hours in front of 'ee – you aren't going to bust a gut. But here, we get on with, because time is time. A shunt come in, British Rail, and if you aren't loaded you'm gone. We'm bit different here. So goodnight.'

Towards end of that week the captain come to me, he said, 'Here, that feller: he's bloody good bloke, you know. He gone up a gear,' he said. 'Usually, when somebody's under a week's notice, you aren't going to get a pile more out of them. You just as well send 'em home right away, send a week's money too. But he's gone up a notch. I think he'd make a good bloke.' I said, 'Good blokes are hard to come by, I suppose. I shall have to eat bit of crow pie.' I went out, and he was on the gantry again. I climbed up and I said, 'Hullo, boy. Friday,' I said, 'tomorrow morning be last shift'. 'Yeh.' I said, 'You got anything yet?' 'No.' I said, 'Well, you seem to be moved up a notch or two in gear.' 'Well,' he said, 'you upset me. I've always been known as a good workman. You come here and said I wasn't very good. I thought I'd show 'ee before I went.' So I said, 'Well, if you got someone else on Monday, you take it. But if you can't find anything better, you come on Monday and carry on as usual.' He said, 'What about my cards and all, that's come?' I said, 'I shall have to go in wages and eat crow pie, that's all. Tell 'em 'twas all horrible mistake and you'm working on and that's all there is to it.'

So on he come. He wasn't exactly my best worker, but he was lost in the pile of good men.

CHAPTER 5

Domestic and Social Life

The downs, Gunheath.

No Mod Cons

Even in the wartime years – and until the sixties – many of the houses in the clay villages were without basic modern amenities. Laurie Stuthridge:

I was born in my grandfather's house, and eventually Mum and Dad got a council house, a little place called Stepaside between Treviscoe and St Stephens. So we went from a fairly modern house, where you had running water, in this council house, to a little cottage with two and a half acres, five small meadows. No electricity, no running water, no drainage, no anything. But we were able to keep a cow a couple of pigs, a few chicken. I was about ten or eleven at the time. Because [Dad] was too old for the services, he was drafted up to Devonport dockyard, war service. Well that left mother and me. I had a small sister who died at a very young age from pneumonia.

But living up on the downs, up on the moors, every year we used to burn the downs. Why there's such a hue and cry about a small fire on Dartmoor or a fire on the downs, I don't know, because we used to burn the downs every year, deliberately. The gorse, the ferns, the whole lot would burn off, and next year it came again. A lot of the furze bushes were only singed really but it was enough to kill them. They were black, and the local name for these bushes were smutties. We used to go and pick smutties because you can break them, having been dried and singed in the fire, and that was the fuel we used for the copper. Mother milked the cow. I'd think nothing of drinking half a pint or a pint of fresh milk, from the cow, while it was still warm. All this panic now about health!

Yes, we had a radio in the house, but that was only on for a quarter of an hour or so of an evening to hear the news. Saturday night it was *In Town Tonight*, and Sunday evening it used to be on for about half an hour for the Palm Court Orchestra. And that was about it. Because batteries were expensive, and the thing that needed charging, the accumulator – do you remember the old glass battery with a handle? You had two of them, one at the garage being recharged, so once a week that had to be changed. And the small nine-volt grid bias battery – so yes, you couldn't afford to waste battery. We didn't know what it was to have electricity in the house until 1946. Well, I was sixteen then. So it was a paraffin lamp. All my homework was done in lamplight, and reading – I'd go to bed with a candle. There was just the one stove in the house which provided all the heat for the cooking, and you'd sit around that of an evening. Coal, yes. A Cornish range, which had an oven,

and the top was quite hot – you could keep things warm or even boil on there. And the top of the actual fireplace could lift out and you could get what we used to call a smoke jack, put that in, and it was almost an open fire then.

—*Did you also have a fire in the living room?*

That *was* your living room. You may have had a small pantry tacked onto that, where you'd have a wire mesh cupboard to try and keep things cool.

—*So the cooking and the eating and the relaxation was all done in one room?*

That's right.

Life in Karslake

Conditions up in the hilltop village of Karslake – since demolished – were perhaps worse, due to its exposed position. Clayton Roberts:

So there was a lot of dangers. It was dangerous enough walking down to the toilet at the bottom of the garden, because you had your cesspit. There was no sanitation inside at all, no sinks. The bath routine was, Sunday night, tin bath by the Cornish range, the dirtiest one got in last and then it was thrown out into the street, the water, and [the bath] hung back on the wall again. You had a range up there, a Cornish range, and you had a fire in the front room. I lived with my mum and dad; we all lived together with my nan and granddad. I was the only child. They used to spoil me rotten, my grandparents. I can't remember if there was fires in the bedroom, I think there might have been. But it was

Clay village on a wet spring day, March 2000.

always cold, freezing cold. I remember Gran putting wallpaper up with flour and water, as a mix. Bloody brown paper. So, very depressing houses.

—Were they damp inside?

Yes. Couldn't keep wallpaper on the walls. It was freezing cold and damp. With no electric either, they were never properly heated. The communal area was always the kitchen because that's where the range was. Everything was done on the range, all the cooking, drying the clothes. In the evening Granddad used to pull out, when the time was right, packet of chestnuts and we used to roast the chestnuts in the bar of the fire.

It was a funny existence. We're talking sixties, here. It sounds like it could have been the thirties or forties, so I've experienced something which is quite

unique. Cornwall was always a little bit behind the rest of the country. This was before the heady days of tourism, so these little communities were untouched and were in effect a time capsule. Progress eventually changed it because they wanted clay, they wanted the clay that was under the houses. There was a rich deposit there.

Life changed radically for Clayton when the family moved to Bodmin.

Dad was working for SWEB, and he got transferred over to the Bodmin depot so we got a house because he was working in Bodmin. That was enough to put you on the council [housing list]. It was relatively easy to get a council house then, so we moved there. And then we moved into our first house, of our own. I remember having a bath – first time I'd ever seen this bloody

A railway carriage house, still in use, summer 1999.

running water stuff! I got into a right pickle, water over the floor and my hair out here with soap suds!

Railway Carriage Homes

Railway carriage homes were fairly common in the clay country. It sounds a cramped existence, but Les Lean obviously loved it.

It would be 1925, round about there, that [father] put the railway carriages there. There's two railway carriages and then there's about ten foot in between, right back through, where we used to have the living room. In our bedroom we used to have the chain you pull for emergency, 'Penalty for improper use: £5'. Stop the train! The railway carriage was good, because on the door we used to have – we'd pull the windows up – you

had these leather straps, lovely great leather straps. Father used to strop his cut-throat razor on that one, see. When there was something on – about 1930s, they used to have boxing on in the middle of the night in America, Joe Louis and Tommy Farr and all they – we were all in bed, all wind our windows down and listen to en in bed, put the wireless on in the living room. So there was advantages. And we had galvanized roof, lovely galvanized roof, I loved the galvanized roof. I said to missus I would nearly put a bit of galvanize on here, because we used to be in bed and hear it roaring down, the rain, oh lovely. Go off sleep snuggled in. I miss the rain rattling on the roof.

In those freer days, when planning rule were lax, where you lived could simply be the place where you stopped straining to haul a railway carriage up a steep and bendy Cornish hill.

[There were] several railway carriages over Greensplat at that time. Clarence was telling me that they was pulling a railway carriage up through the lane there by Greensplat Chapel, and they couldn't turn the corner up top. So this bloke come along, he said, 'Well, that don't matter. Put it down the bottom.' They put en in over the hedge and kept en there, lived there. They didn't worry so much then.

Killing the Pig

Pig slaughter in those days of a generation or two ago was partly a survival necessity, partly an entertainment – particularly for the children. Arthur and Glenda Bullock remember how it used to be done at Foxhole.

Arthur: In our early days nearly everybody kept a pig, and then when he's fat enough Mart Dalley would come down and we'd tie it on a wood bench stock and he'd cut their throat. Then we'd hang it up. All his insides we'd take down to the – what we call the chute, which is the water chute, there's a natural chute – and we'd take it all down there and we'd wash it, wash all his insides out. They'd make nattlings and girtymeat and all sorts of dishes that the poor people could eat. It was delicious. Then we'd hang the rest of the pig, and that one would last us until the next pig would come on. All our old potato skins, turnip skins and all the rubbish like, was all for the pig. A neighbour would come on, 'I'm killing pig, but we don't want the stomach, do you want en?' 'Oh yes please'. We'd go down with one of they old galvanized baths, and rake it in there and take it up to the chute and wash all the insides out. You know just how filthy that is. And then on he'd go, and he'd be cackling

The remains of a railway carriage home, Greensplat, spring 2000.

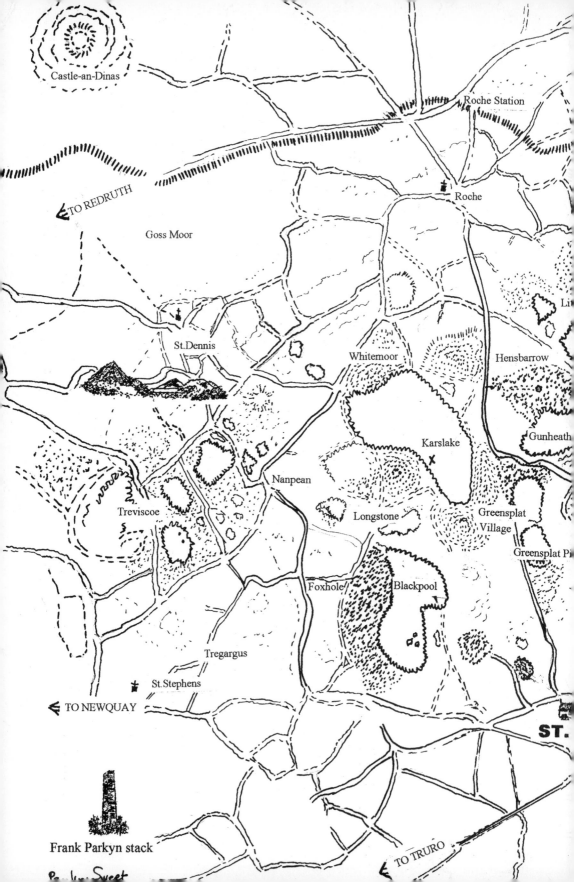

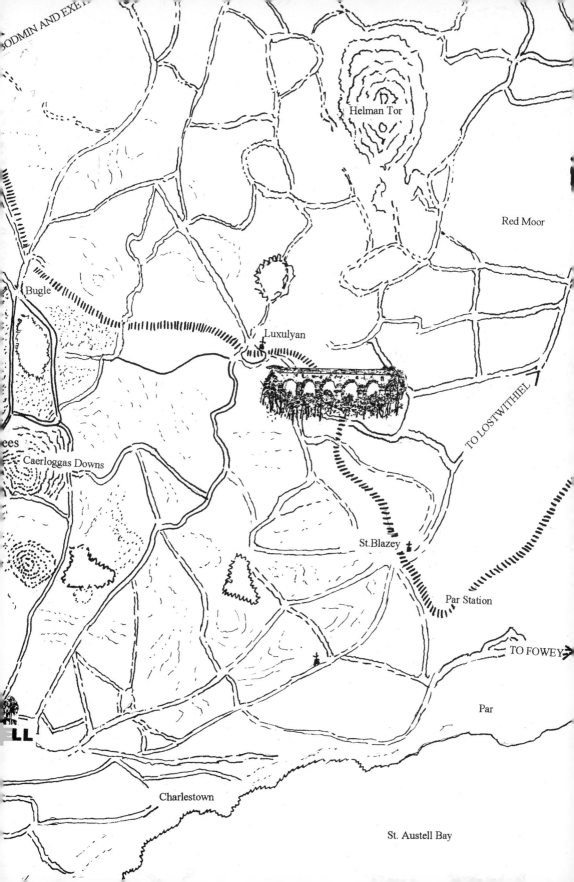

Arthur Bullock with Martin, 1982.

Glenda Bullock.

away on the blacklead stove, in the old boiler. Cor – we had some lovely dishes out of that. The pig's head – they used to take out the eyes, they never put the eyes in – but all the rest of it went in and make some brawn. Brawn was lovely. Home-made brawn. Nearly every night you could hear screaming pig somewhere, somebody was killing a pig.

Glenda: Everybody congregated and watched it. It was horrible. I used to be like this [hands over ears] because the pig would scream, oh dreadful.

Arthur: They get the pig and tie en to the stock, it was just like a wood stretcher.

Glenda: It didn't get stunned or anything.

Arthur: They just tie en down. Then he'd [the slaughterman] go up and he'd mark en with the knife. Then a bit more – and that pig is really screaming – and then they'd cut en and then -cheeooo – they cut his throat. Cut his windpipe. Then he's dead.

—Did you help with the pig killing?

Arthur: We did. We had to. Boys had to.

Glenda: After he was killed, I used to help then – have the scraper and scrape his skin.

Arthur: You scrape all the hair off.

Glenda: I can't remember it, but apparently I went out and caught my gran cleaning the pigs pots, as they called 'em – the stomach and the intestines – and I never would touch sausages after that, for years and years.

Arthur: And the chicken. 'We'll have a chicken for Sunday.' Right, pick up the chicken and bring en in. Tie his legs – they tie en to the clothes line. Hang it up – and then they'd have a knife....in his beak, right back in his throat, and cut the artery on the back of his throat. Then he would bleed. And he'd kick, kick, kick – and all the blood's gone then. The blood would all fly out.

Glenda: I can't bear that. He bled to death. He was hours hung by the feet.

Arthur: Not for a chicken; chicken didn't take long. Ten minutes, the chicken was dead. Some used to cut his head off, but they still hang en up and he'd be going for ten minutes there, flicking round on the clothes line. Flapping his wings and that. All the blood's gone then. Five or ten minutes, the pig would die. But he suffered.

—Was he squealing all that time?

Oh yes he's squealing all right.

Glenda: In some ways 'twas a kind of a community thing. All the children went. 'Mr So-and-so's killing pig, come on.' They would say, 'Here, we don't want the head – you want to make a bit of brawn, you can have that one. You can have the stomach.'

Urts

Up on the downs between the pits and the dries, there was a free harvest to be gathered.

Arthur: Summertime you got to pick blackberries first, or else you got to go out pick urts. We call em urts, but 'tis whortleberries. There's loads of 'em up on the downs. Still up there. Nobody pick 'em now. We used to go up, the whole family. 'We'll all go up tonight, pick urts'. They was only little small ones. We used to make tarts, and they were beautiful. Urty tart they used to call 'em. And milk we used to have. We used to put it on the blacklead stove overnight and then we get the cream, make your own cream. You drink the scalded milk then, like ordinary. But the cream – we used to make urty tart and blackberry tart or apple tart. We used to make loads of blackberry jam or blackberry and apple jam.

Glenda: [Urts are] so soft and juicy that they don't need much cooking. Simmer 'em for ten minutes.

Arthur: Everybody had an enamel plate, like a dinner plate. They'd put 'em in there and put a cover of pastry on the top. I don't know of anybody now make urty tart. They can't be bothered go up there pick 'em. Urts are so small. If we found a good place and you'd filled your jar, we used to have a piece of grass, long grass, and thread em up on it. Stalk of dried grass, and then thread 'em up through. Call 'em what 'ee like; that's what we used to call em: urty tart.

Owning the Land

Many clay-workers lived in houses owned by the clay company, or which were on land owned by the company – which retained its right to use this land for tipping or clay extraction. So life could sometimes seem insecure. Clarence Hancock – living right next to Greensplat pit…
—I suppose the clay company could burrow under this house to get at more clay – because they hold the mineral rights.

Clarence Hancock's house, Greensplat, 1999.

That's right. They could order we out any time, because our house stands on freehold of two feet. Beyond that is a mineral right. A lot of houses have been knocked down because of the fact that the clay companies wanted to go through that way. Yes, there used to be quite a few houses over Halviggan. All they were buried up, or gone in the pits. If they didn't want it for clay they want it for burrow, tipping ground.

—Did the company rehouse these people?

Not officially. They all found their own places, either through the councils or buy something themselves. I don't know of anywhere, in the latter years, where the clay company was held responsible for finding a house for them. Course, Restormel Council and the clay company have worked together a heck of a lot for to get these things done.

A lot of people from up Karslake went up Roche to live. Others went down round St Stephens and Nanpean. 'Twas done because of circumstances. Somehow or another they managed it, and the people would fall in line.

Mineral rights were not always held by the large clay companies. In times past, individuals and families could sometimes claim mineral extraction royalties.

Our family was all Foxhole. My grandfather and his father owned the whole of Foxhole on this side of the road, and this is the side with all the china clay. They owned the royalties and the rights of all this, but when Fortescue and they came along, [the family] were too small to fight, and [Fortescue] took over the china clay. Wasn't enough go in us, to say, 'Hang on, that's ours.' We sold all the land, and the clay underneath came out after. We lost all the royalties. We weren't big enough to fight 'em.

AB

Class and Society

The Cornish tend to treat all people the same; you either get on with them, or you are free to take yourself off back up-country! It is perhaps partly a Celtic way of doing things, reinforced by the non-conformist religious attitudes popularized by the Wesley brothers in the eighteenth century. Bob…

Pre-war, we were middle class. We had servants in the house and once a week, woman come in do the rough work. The war buggered us because father contributed all he could to the war effort because he believed in it, then after the war everybody else caught up and the differential went. Now, basically we're all middle class aren't we, if you use pre-war standards as your yardstick.

Charles Wesley went through, brought Methodism. Well, Methodists relied heavily on lay preachers, so you might find a feller that's captain all the week is actually in the Bible class of one of his labourers on Sunday. And neither of them felt embarrassed, or that it was incongruous. One was boss man as far as clay was concerned, the other was boss man as far as God was concerned. Although there was poor and rich, and highly thought of labourers and labourers that weren't worth spit, it didn't feel like class. As a kid I would come in, and I might see Selleck, director of a company, sitting and having a whisky with father in the dining room, or I might see Harry Kendall,

the mica man from up north, sitting down in a corner having a cup of tea or a beer, and chatting over with father. Because that where [father's] knowledge, background and what he was doing, come from. If you don't understand the rudiments of your business you can't really do it. I would be equally polite to both or have a bloody good hiding from Mother. Mother always gave us an alternative; you could do what you was told first time, or have a hiding and do it second time. You could suit yourself, but do it.

In Bob's middle-class home, living conditions were better than in some. But Mother was strict, and lessons in social attitudes were painfully learnt by young Bob.

There was an old chap that lived over the road on a lane down to Wheal Henry lane. We knew he lived there, but I hadn't seen him before. One day, it was a nice sunny day, he was outside his back door sitting on a kitchen chair. And he was an old chap then, and we called it Lively's Lane. I came home and I said, 'I seen old man Lively today sitting out in the sun.' Mother put the stick on my legs. I said, 'What was that for?' She said, 'He's Mister Lively to you and don't you ever forget it. We do live like fighting cocks, and 'tis the Mister Livelys of this world that put the grub on your table.' I said, 'Well, everybody call him old man…' 'I don't care what everybody do. He's Mister Lively to you. That's the end of that.'

Mother decided that I would go up and stay with relations in Paignton, and go to Totnes Grammar School instead of here, because she'd come around the corner one day when I'm about ten or eleven years old, and found my foot up on a chair and a housemaid doing up my shoelaces. Course, mother – nearly ballistic! 'What's going on here then?' The maid said, 'Well he was taking so long to do up his shoelaces, I said I'd do 'em up for him.' She said, 'Yes, that's all right, I ain't blaming you. But when he's a man he'll still be a proper shit if 'tis left to people like you doing up his bootlaces.' She said, 'I'll fix you, my son, you needn't worry about that.' No more said. Next thing I knew I was booked in Totnes Grammar School. She said, 'You go up there and find out how rough life can be. You'll appreciate your home when you come home on holiday.' And I did too.

Everyone I have ever spoken to about life in Britain before about 1960 has said that there was much less crime and a much greater sense of social responsibility. So perhaps it is true, and not a rainbow effect produced by nostalgia. Laurie Stuthridge talks about his home village:

There were one or two people that were a little simple, that might do something a bit daft, but there was certainly no violent crimes, not out in the villages. The police knew everybody. I cannot honestly recollect any cases of housebreaking or.... Things used to be stolen from the works, but you'd get that anyway. Someone takes some copper wire – but the police knew almost immediately because word would get around that so-and-so's suddenly come into money. No, I think people were basically honest, and were afraid of the consequences of breaking the law.. Plus the fact that you had your own self-respect within the community. In the smaller villages, everyone knew everyone else by their first name. They knew who their father had married and where she came from, and probably knew her parents.

My parents were never in debt. Never very

flush. Dad came home with his pay packet and he'd give it to Mum, and in the big glass dresser there would be different tea pots and jugs, and there would be what was for the groceries in one, what was for the rent in another, what was for the rates in another. If they were saving for something, if dad needed a new suit or coat or mother need a new coat, what was to spare would go back in there, maybe a couple of bob. Latterly, they had a holiday, one week on the Scilly Isles. They would spend a whole year saving up for that one week. That was the highlight of their life. Dad used to smoke, so mother bought the tobacco – because he used to roll his own – she would buy that in with the groceries, so he'd get his one or two packets of tobacco a week. Maybe about once a month he would go down to the pub in St Stephens, have a couple of bottles of Guinness, and back up again. That would come out of the kitty. But that kitty was only there after everything else had been provided for.

An Isolated Village

Clayton Roberts remembers a similar sense of social cohesion in the vanished village of Karslake.

There was twenty-four houses in a row. On the moors.

—*Sounds really isolated.*

It was. But the community there, they all looked out for each other. Dad was one of the few that had a car, so he used to take a lot of people to work with him in the morning. There was one person who had a telephone. [He] was a charge-hand in the pit, and they put a phone in for him, so he always had a

Clayton's grandmother, aged eighty in 1997. She shared the Karslake home.

queue at his door. The nearest payphone was at Old Pound – you had to walk several miles. A lady called Kitty Dingle had a little shop up there, like a galvanized shack. Just serving twenty-four houses – which worked very well. And then there was a guy down at Carthew called Mr Abbott who run the little shop down there. He would come up, take everybody's orders, and everybody had tick off Mr Abbott. He'd also install these cigarette machines, little wood boxes. You put your money in and get your cigarettes out. Every house had a little cigarette box machine, because times were hard. He used to do a roaring trade up there.

It sounds too good to last. It was....

I took Sal up to see it when we were about sixteen, seventeen, and the houses were standing then, but they were all empty so it was a bit like a ghost town, very eerie. Of course this happened to many hamlets round. Old Pound, for instance. The clay took over, so these little communities were eventually disbanded.

—So as the pits encroached, the settlements had to go?

That's right, yep. And they just went in there with a bulldozer and flattened it. I think it was Ray – lives out at Foxhole – done the deed, and – pfft! – put the dozer in gear and just flattened the houses. This happened with a lot of hamlets in the clay area. [The clay companies] bought the houses, or had the houses built; they were used for many years, and then people were offered alternative accommodation. Obviously they didn't kick

Clayton as tacker, with the pipe, at Karslake.

people out. They bought other houses in different areas, and people went to live there. The community scattered. It was a rough crowd, but a bloody good crowd. They were lovely people. It was rough and ready. It was a hard place to live. You were up, nearly the highest place ...might have been *the* highest occupied place in Cornwall. Right up on the moors, on the downs. There was a bus service, but in the snow you were cut off. I remember quite vividly, in the 1960s there was a hell of a snowstorm; we were cut off up there for days. The community spirit, I've never witnessed it since. As kids, you'd be in and out of peoples' houses, and you'd have dinner there. There were some black children up there as well, which I never took any notice of. Because of the war, they actually stationed, Dad was saying, a black marine corps up there, because

they were segregated. The black marines weren't allowed to camp at the same places. So there was one or two mixed-race children.

Not that everyone was perfect – not even Clayton!

My aunty Mabel – she was married to my granddad's brother, she was a second aunty really – to keep me quiet – because I must have been a right little tearaway when I was a kid, they used to give me some money to go down and get flour and water and make up bread. And they'd give me a cigarette to smoke; woody Woodbine, four year old this is. And my granddad, in the evenings, to keep me quiet would give me a tot of whisky so Id fall asleep with my milk [Laughs]. Four years old, I was smoking. Not on a full-time basis, but I'd be there making the pastry, smoking a fag. And this wasn't seen to be any... it was a laugh. This little blond-haired, curly-headed kid, rolling this pastry up smoking this fag and drinking my granddad's scotch – bloody amazing.

—*Was it a hard swearing society?*

Oh, definitely. I learnt how to swear as soon as I learnt how to talk. I didn't realize any different because everybody swore. It wasn't a case that I was trying to be rude, it was a part of my vocabulary, which I learnt how to express myself.

—*And the social network extended down into the pit...*
I never realized how much until Dad talked about it; who was related to who. When I

first started with ECLP, I went down into the pit onto the hose. There was one guy up at the top of the pit that I didn't go much on, he was a bit abrupt. I was down in the pit and they said, 'Who are you?' I said, 'Clayton Roberts'. 'Oh yeah, you Clar's boy?' I said, 'Yes, that's right.' Talking for an hour or so on the hose, and I said, 'God, matey's a right miserable sod, up there.' 'Who's that, boy?' 'Oh, matey up there, what's he called...?' He said, 'That's my bloody brother, but I agree with you, he is a miserable bugger!'

Greensplat

Les Lean remembers how three threads of clay country society – chapel, brass bands, and the patronage of the pit-owning families – sometimes intertwined.

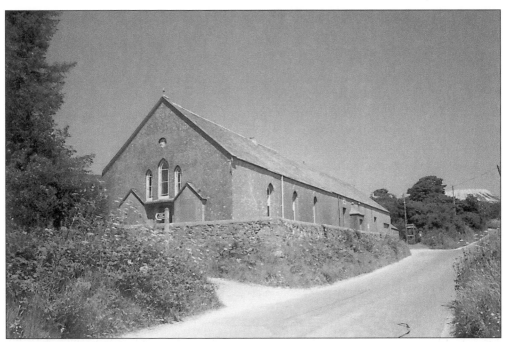

Greensplat chapel, 1999.

Back long, the chapel was the centre – to us – we had nothing else, never went nowhere else more than chapel and choir practice, band practice. Nothing else up there doing. When I joined the choir, when I was about fourteen or fifteen, I loved it. Loved it. 'Twas lonely, walking home to Hensbarrow over Greensplat. Dark. No lights on, no nothing. No street lights, no lights in the clay works. End of the war, there. Hell, with the galvanized rattle, I used to be scared stiff. Couldn't see nothing. Feel your way along the hedge. Up Greensplat, we used to have the band there sometimes, and march up and down. Used to march in Carthew house. All that's gone now. The clay works is in Carthew House. There was a lovely big house in there. The Martyns used to own all the land up round there, and they used to do a lot for Greensplat chapel. I've had the books here and have read about Martyn. [The chapel] used to borrow some money off them and then pay it back. When they built the new Sunday School, they had a lot of money off the Martyn family, and then paid them back – Miss Ivy. We used to go in Carthew House with the band, and all go on the lawns. They used to throw us sweets out on the lawns – pick up. If you go up by the chapel, look across the pit, you see the remains of a house now, and that was Mr Alford, used to be the gamekeeper and carpenter. Still the remains of that house there now. And up Wheal Martyn drive, all that led up to the big house – beside the museum, yes.

Access

The downs have always been criss-crossed by workmen's pathways – not all of which survive (q.v. Peter Bishop, below).

All the people from Greensplat used to come down the lovely pathway coming from Greensplat, come out past Wheal Martyn by the museum. The bus used to stop at the gates there, Wheal Martyn gates, and they used to walk up through from there, up to Greensplat. Then down across Blackberry Row the other side, a path up there. Took away the pathway, they haven't replaced it.

Some of the old customs have also disappeared, perhaps fortunately.

Father said, there at Old Pound, if any chaps came from other places come up there and tried take away their girls, they used to pick up tabs, turf, aim at them and drive them away. Wouldn't let them have their girls. But 'twas a simple way of life back years ago.

LL

A Clay Town

Like all communities in the clay area, St Blazey has been shaped by its association with the clay industry. Malcolm Bowers:

St Blazey really was a town at one time. With fifty shops you could say yes, it was. From what the older people tell me, people came out. If they didn't go to St Austell on a Saturday they came out to St Blazey to do their shopping, and they could get anything they wanted here. There were clothes shops, the Co-op had shops here, the International Stores had shops here. All the way down the main street. And when it happened that ECC wanted the road widening for their big lorries, those were just pulled down. They took the heart out of the place really. They even took some of the churchyard away, in the early seventies. Shops were probably closing by then, but all those shops were knocked down to widen the road.

St Blazey did have a bit of a reputation. Things have got better in the last few years. If you look at the crime statistics, they have improved. But it is basically a working-class parish. The [private] estate up the road – people go there but many don't stay there, not because they're not nice little houses but it's the first step on the ladder. It's a small house, say two bedrooms, and when the family comes along they want another step up the ladder and want to go. Now, that doesn't help the community either because they're really not interested in getting involved.

Put it this way, the vast majority are local. That wouldn't apply to many parish churches in Cornwall, somewhere like Budock for instance. I would say they will have their indigenous population but a lot will be retired people. The retired don't come here to live. They go to the places they consider more attractive, so we haven't got the incoming retired people, or like Truro, incoming business people, or people who work in the hospital. Not many surgeons in Trelisk are going to be living in St Blazey. They might commute ten or twelve miles to work, but they're going to be living in places like Budock down near Falmouth. Places that are more desirable. St Blazey's at the bottom end of the market, housing-wise.

—The parishioners who actually attend church – are they typical of a Cornish village congregation?

I think, with Cornish people, if you minister to them, if you love them, if you enter into their society and families and get to know

Malcolm Bowers.

them and their community, and be a part of that community, then they'll go to hell or high water for you. If you rub them up the wrong way, then you've got problems. Got to take it gently and let them get to know you, and you to know them. You've got to get to know your parish and to know the people in it. Not necessarily all by name. They must see you around.

[The vicarage] was a coaching house for the Carlyons at Tregrehan, one of the big landowners round here. One of their number became a vicar and they turned it into a vicarage. It's 1834 or something, outside on top of one of the drainpipes, but whether that's the actual age of the place I don't know. Certainly it's early Victorian if not older. It's build with granite and Pentewan stone, which is quite soft stuff – that reddy stone you see in so many buildings round here. All sorts of bits have been added on.

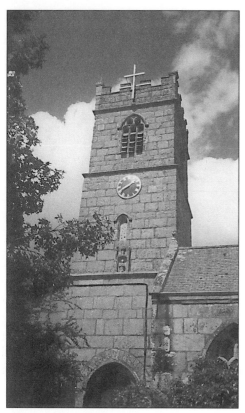

The church, St Blazey.

Technology Moves On

Technology moves on, jobs go, a community has to change. Colin Cloke saw it happen.

St Blazey's declined, yes. Because steam went, so your railway sheds went. Employment that was in Par sheds – remarkably high. You were either a clay worker or a railway worker or down on the docks. You couldn't really say that they were separate. They were all depending on each other. A lot of your clay-works and dries were on the harbour, which was convenient for the railways because the railway line went right down on the harbour. It still does, but it's not open like it used to be.

When you go the back of the Moor you'll see a bridge with five arches, that granite bridge. You look at them. One goes over the canal, one goes over the railway line and one goes over the road, all heading for Par harbour.

When you got rid of steam you didn't need people to light fires, to clean the ashes out. A steam engine took a hell of a lot of maintenance for what you got out of it, whereas a diesel, you switch him off at the end of the day, and tomorrow morning you just go in and check the oil.

—With all these steam engines around, Par in the old days must have been full of the noise of…

Railway engines. Everywhere. Hooters going, yeah!

On Benefit

The old ways could be brutal ways. The means tests, back in the earlier years of the twentieth century, were notoriously inhumane. George Morcom:

My father had died when I was eight year old. After the first war the men started paying what was known as 'Lloyd George'. It was insurance – but they weren't going to pay out until 1926, so when father died at 1924 there was nothing for you more than parish pay. At the time, someone had to recommend you for parish pay. The doctor came in – back at they days where anybody had died and the wife was left they would come round and just see how the wife was going on – and when he came the parson was just going out. So he came in and he said, 'Oh, the parson been in and wrote the letter to the board of guardians I suppose'. 'No', mother said. 'But he did tell me, "Don't you worry, Mrs Morcom, the Lord will provide!"'

[The doctor] said, 'I'll write the letter'. So he wrote the letter, and there was a man called Medland Stocker – he was a big man in the clay-works, he was one of the head ones of the board of guardians – so he had to come. At the time you had to be, how shall I put it... you had to be destitute. He said to mother, 'Now, you're four in the family. If you've got five chairs you've got to get rid of one.' He said, 'The first question is, Have you any money? No. Now,' he said, 'we've answered that question, we shan't have no trouble now.' So he made out the application. Consequently mother had the parish pay. Back at that time you were looked down upon if you had parish pay. There used to be a man used to come round with a landau from St Austell, and he had a man driving this landau, and he come in with this black bag and he used to dish out mother 26s for four of us.

1926 they started paying the widows and orphans pension, which was something similar. Mother then had a pension book, and she was made, because she could go down post office. The money wasn't really enough to keep us, so mother used to go out to work and wash clothes for people.

Kids and Territories

Sue Hill gained insight into Clay Country life when she worked on a theatre project near Foxhole in the summer of 1999.

I was born in Penzance and grew up in Redruth, so I'm not a clay girl. Carn Brea was my patch, my playground. We used to go and stand on Carn Brea, and in those days you could look east from Carn Brea and you could see these beautiful white pyramids, 'Cornish Alps'. Of course you cant see them any more because they've all been landscaped. The clay was like another country. We never went there. Foreign land.

—*Was that mutual?*

Yep, I'm sure. Very tribal. Absolutely. You stuck to your own – and there's still a sense of that in some ways. The clay has kept that, whereas I think Redruth, Camborne, that's less true now, because – mainly – loss of the focusing power of employment. When I was growing up, Redruth and Camborne were still major engineering centres. Every week you could see these great trucks roll out from Holme and Climax carrying compressors, sending compressors off around the world to.... Everywhere there was a hole in the ground, this fantastic machinery would be.... But that's gone, and the confidence has gone. There's not that sense of confidence and focus and ownership any more, in those communities. But I think there is still in the clay – well I know there is in the clay – still.

We knew [the Hendra pit theatre project] was going to be more of a challenge than some of the other residency work we'd done because it was such a strong community, and in some senses quite a closed community, and not a particularly arts-based community. It seemed to be quite clear from our contact with the clay, and from people who lived and worked there, that arty-farty was somewhere you didn't want to go, really.

We looked for stories in the youth club and they came up with this fantastic story

The foreign land – the northern edge in the Indian Queens area, 1982. [EN]

about buried villages. Apparently there are a number, the most famous of which is called Retin. The kids generated this idea of the ghosts of the villages, the people who had lived in the villages that were now buried. For their carnival at Nanpean they made a ghost procession with these huge figures – white, spooky, very beautiful ghost figures. And they were inordinately proud of this. They did it in the Nanpean carnival, and they won two prizes and they won a £5 note as well. They were so excited by this they had to go in the St Dennis carnival and they won two prizes again, and another £5.

There are all kind of territorial battles going on in the clay. Everyone said to us, 'They're wild people up there, they're indians. Your marquee'll be torched. You can't leave anything unattended, it'll be nicked. You'll have to watch everything. No respect for property.' So we went in with a certain amount of trepidation. On the first night that we were there, the indians arrived on top of the hill – loads of boys on bikes – and they kind of milled around on top of the hill like that scene in *Zulu*. They didn't get any closer, and at night there were a few stones thrown at the tent. But over the next three days they got closer and closer to the tent and by the end of the third day they were sitting on the sofa, in the tent, drinking coffee. It became very clear that there are two tribes operating there. The indians are one, and the landies – what they call the land-rover people – are the others. And there's a sense in which they're in a battle for the right to use the land.

The Hendra pit project, 1999. 'Arrie' and his brother Jonathan, after a performance, with their giant puppet.

Clay country life has always been tough, as we have seen. But the toughness now is different, especially among the young people. Perhaps this is because of the changes in the industry itself. Jobs are no longer assured, and the unemployment rate is high. Sue Hill again:

There is intense poverty in the clay, and there's a lot of subsistence burglary. You nick your neighbour's lawnmower and flog it in the boot sale down the road. There's also a deal of frustration and boredom, so there's a lot of joyriding. Kids'll nick cars and drive them up to Hendra pit and torch them. But they're not evil people. That's the way the situation polarizes into – Those are *bad* people, and these are *good* people. They're kids. And they're kids who want to ... they want to be entertained. Actually they want to have some fun. And to have a great big marquee arrive on site.... I think what became clear is, there was more fun to be had by not torching the marquee than by torching it.

The Students' View

Four students – Claire, Jamie, Tim and Richard – at St Austell College give their version of what it is like for young people, living in the clay villages in the new millennium.

Claire: It's looked down upon, living in the village, I think. Like Bugle and Penwithick, Roche, Stenalees, anywhere like that. As soon as you mention that you live in one of the villages it's almost frowned upon. You're the butt of everybody's jokes.

Jamie: It's surprising how many people don't actually know about the villages which lie around St Austell. You say you live in

Foxhole, and they say, Oh, where's that?

Claire: I suppose it's different growing up in a little village than it is growing up in St Austell. You're stuck out on a limb in a village; you get to spend a lot more time at home, whereas when my friends were growing up they were out all the time. They had all their friends, and they had all the amenities and everything there, close by. I don't have any friends in Roche now; all my friends are in St Austell. All the people that I went to primary school with are still in Roche, they're still hanging around on the street corners. They don't really do a lot any more. They all seem to be stuck in a rut there. A little gathering of them outside the bakery in the evening, and they're all there. Five or six years on they're all still doing the same thing.

Jamie: I want to go to university and study medicine, so nothing to do with the clay industry. I would like to come back to Cornwall, set up a nice family practice. I just like the area. All my family and friends are around here. It's more a community-orientated area, Cornwall. Up in London, if you'd had a GP practice you wouldn't really know the patients as well as if you're from a small community.

Tim: Ideally I'd like to stay around here, but looks as if, if I want work, I'm going to have to go somewhere else and find it. I'll have to go away and train for it.

—But you'd come back?

Yes. I like it around here. I been brought up here – I suppose I don't know any different.

Richard: I want to do something in computers and management. I'll probably go away for a university, and I don't know if I'll come back or not, because my brother and my sister have gone away to university – they don't want to come back. They say its a totally different life up there. Its faster. More stuff up there.

—*Would that attract you?*

I don't know yet.

Claire: I do think I'll probably end up coming back here to start a family. I'd like the children to grow up in Cornwall. I think it's safer. That's why my parents moved down here. They loved coming down to Cornwall on holidays, and when I was born – my parents are from Liverpool and they didn't want me growing up, up there. I am glad that I grew

up down here but I just feel I want a bit more now. I had a whale of a time when I was younger, because we used to live near some woods and the clay pits and everything. It's brilliant if you're a little kid, you can roam round everywhere – but you do get tired of it after a while.

—*What's attracting you to go elsewhere?*

More opportunities. Jobs. Education. It's lovely here, but not lovely enough.

Tim: I prefer a bit more of a mix. I think there's too much countryside. Sometimes you see in these cities they've got better facilities.

Claire: A few of my friends travelled down from up-country to see some other friends

The pretty end of a Clay village: St Dennis.

Roche – the rock and St Michael's chapel perched on the top.

that live close by, and they drove through Roche. All they could say about it was, 'Saw where you live. It's a bit grim isn't it!' Cornwall is really beautiful, but I think the clay villages could be a lot more, if they were made to look a bit prettier. It's an important part. There are so many people that are involved in the clay industry.

—What would improve life in Cornwall for young people?

Tim: Better job opportunities. Possibly a university down here – encourage people to stay here longer.

—If there were a university, where should it be sited?

Claire: Roche, yes. [Laughter]

The Changing Village

Village life in Foxhole, once a working community, is undergoing changes. Arthur Bullock:

The recreation ground – we had a half pipe made for 'em, for their skateboards and their bikes. There's a bowling alley out there, there's table tennis. I've done a great big area tarmacked out, for their skateboards, for basketball. The young children, they got a super play area but they're absolutely wrecking it. At the moment there's a crowd of them out there. I should imagine they were bored. They can't utilize nothing, teenagers. 'Tis a pity, really.

—Is the village changing?

It's changing now. There's not a lot of Cornish people left. There's a lot of up-country ones even in our block here. They sell their house up the country for big money, so they can buy something cheap down here. They buy a lovely car and they can go Newquay, half an hour to Newquay, ten minutes to St Austell, twenty minutes to Mevagissey.

—*So it doesn't matter that Foxhole's not very pretty itself?*

Its only a base.

Mevagissey Feast Week

Social life in Mevagissey has changed.

No matter where you were, if possible you always came home for Mevagissey feast week.

Each church or denomination had their feast day. All in one week. There'd be a band, and different churches would march around the town and stop at different points in the village and sing their anniversary hymns. Then they'd all go back to the recreation field for tea and sports. On the Sunday it started, it used to be the Church of England, their afternoon, and the Congregationalists – there was two that afternoon. The Wednesday was the Wesleyans, and then the United Methodists was the Friday.

The Saturday was the Carnival day, sports and different things on the field. A whole week the town would be decorated, which it is still – not to the extent that it

Sunday School banners at Mevagissey Feast week parade.

United Methodists children's feast, Mevagissey, 1948.

The Procession, Mevagissey Feast Week, 2000.

was then. And all the fishermen would finish fishing on the Monday or Tuesday of that week, and they'd stay in the harbour and all their boats would be decorated with flags. It was a real celebration, St Peter's tide. I think it's the last Sunday in June [St Peter's day is 29 June]. And then late at night, after the pubs shut, a lot of the men – there was some lovely, lovely singers, Mevagissey always had a lovely male voice choir – they would congregate in the square and sing all the hymns. They would go on until well after midnight.

—Do they still do that?

Not as much, no. And there's always that element now of rowdiness with it. You get perhaps twenty, thirty police in Mevva Saturday night now, of a feast week – and the police dogs. You didn't need them in those days.

CS

The Rabbit Catcher

One hundred-year-old Jim Ellery's memory stretches across the decades to recalls snatches of verse. Both he and his father earned their livings as rabbit catchers.
—Did you eat rabbit yourself?

Occasionally yes. We didn't sicken ourselves, of course, we didn't need to. We had a fowl or two...

Jim Ellery aged 100 years 7 months, summer 2000.

Class of 1908 at Talskiddy. Jim Ellery is on the front row, at the extreme right.

...flesh is good to eat
And 'twill make us big and strong.

Breaking up,
Going away,
For our summer's holiday....
You've heard that, have 'ee?
No more slates,
No more books
No more teacher's ... (then we say teacher's name)... so and so's ugly looks.
There was one [teacher] called Maud Powell. They didn't care for she, she was a bit strict. She give 'ee a little tap on the leg with a cane.

—Did you sometimes catch the wrong animal by mistake in your gin traps?

You want to catch me out, I can see that!

—No I don't [we laugh]. Did you ever catch a fox?

My father might say, it takes a gale of wind, a shower of rain and a starshoot to catch a fox. They're so cunning and they have so keen smell that they wouldn't be able to catch a fox. It takes a shower of rain – wash out their.... We like the shower of rain, better for catching rabbits even – a gale of wind – blow your scent away – and a starshoot – make the old fox jump, he wouldn't look where he was going.

Talking to his daughter Joy he recalls chapel anniversary celebrations:

Joy: That was a great occasion, the anniversary.

Jim: It was a great occasion. Lots of people

turn up from in town. Sunday School come out from Nine Maidens even, children from Middle Lamb. They kept the seats, little tiny trestles and long thick planks, over Rosedinnick – and the tables. Kept it over there in the barn up in the beams. Used to bring it over in a wagon, and they'd leave the wagon here for the preacher to preach from, the Sunday.

Joy: And they'd push the organ up through the village?

Jim: In a trap. We didn't have the pony but we had the trap The organ was some heavy to take out from down chapel, had to lift it up over the pews. [The band would go] in through the workhouse grounds, stay and play a tune there in front of the – ever been in there? There's an archway there – and

'twas pathetic really, because some of the poor things, when we went in there, would start to cry. Band playing – the poor things – be in tears.

[After the anniversary tea] the band would form up and march over the road, and they would have – walk around what they call a serpentine walk. Had a big flag. You'd be walking like a snake, in and around – and you'd be meeting – you'd be going there, and you'd be passing – and they'd be coming here, eventually – winding around.

Talskiddy early last century.

CHAPTER 6

Time Off: Leisure and Chapel

Greensplat Chapel band, outside the chapel. The date is unknown.

Going Shooting

'...We made our own fun'. A cliché, but like most clichés, quite true.

From the age of fourteen I had a shotgun. In fact nearly every household had shotguns in those days. Saturday afternoons we would go out. If you had a chance of a wood pigeon or a woodcock, fine, but it was mainly rabbits. The aim was really to get four if we could,

two that we would sell to the butcher for a shilling each, that would more or less cover the cost of the cartridges, and two you'd keep. We had a loose arrangement with the owner of the local corn mill down at Kernick. Yes, we could shoot on his land. We didn't pay him, but by arrangement with one or two of the farmers – they were glad to have the rabbits kept down anyway, and occasionally if you give them one or two rabbits, if you'd got a few, it worked out quite amicably. There would be two big hunting days, Good Friday and Boxing Day. That would be when families would get together and go out as a gang of about six or eight, each with guns, couple of dogs, ferrets – and come back with perhaps as many as twenty between you.

LS

Country Music

—*Was there any music up at Karslake – a band?*

I can't remember no music. I was brought up on a mixture of Slim Whitman and Jim Reeves. Everybody liked country music – and Elvis Presley. So there was always these things playing in every house. Every time I hear a Jim Reeves record, especially *Welcome to my World*, it clicks immediately. Mother was a great fan of all these country stars, Tammy Winette. So all this country music has always stayed there – and rock and roll, I was always into rock and roll, Buddy Holly – very much a romantic-type person, in respects of music. My kids call it 'I kicked my dog' music. All these old country and western ballads, which I hold with very, very fond memories because of Mum. She loved the music. She'd sing away... and there was a woman up there – Brenda, Bren. She and my mum was lifetime friends. Beautiful voice. She's still like it to this day, she sings, and away she goes. So that was the musical culture. You could hear Brenda singing a mile off. Even to this day Brenda'll go up on a stage and pick up a microphone and off she'll go. She got a lovely voice.

CR

Brass Bands

Les Lean's railway carriage home seems to have been a brass band centre. I was not sure how this worked out in practice.
—*What instrument did you play in the band?*

On the big one I used to play the double B, and then the G trombone, the one with the handle. I played with Greensplat band and Penwithick and Mount Charles and finished up with Stenalees. Four boys in the band. My sister used to play the organ up at Greensplat chapel.

—*Did you have music lessons?*

No, no. Nothing like that. Father was a bandmaster. You used to start off.... I remember him... he had a hymn tune there, [sings] 'Jesus high and glory, lend a listening ear'. I remember that hymn tune now. He'd put the fingering on that, first and third, first and second, all like that. Right. You played that hymn tune off, and then you knew where the fingering was, on the notes, on the music. Never had no teaching. Brother and me taught the same time, with a hymn tune like that. You pick it up. You know, that's a D, first and third. E is first and second, and F is first valve....He never taught us no music, never no teaching.

—*That railway carriage must have been a noisy place on band practice nights.*

But mother didn't mind. Mother was a lovely woman. She would stick all that if we was happy. She was happy as a lark with us doing things like that. We used to have others come up as well, some from Greensplat come up our place, the same age as us, practising, play with us.

Jim Ellery, 1908.

'Rugby Without Rules'

As a young man Jim Ellery took part in the traditional St Columb rough and tumble game played with a silver ball. It's like rugby without the benefit of referee or rulebook.
—*In St Columb they have this game…*

Hurling.

—*Did you take part in that?*

Anybody can. You could. You can't take [the silver ball] out the parish. Course, some places it's a long way to get out the parish. The nearest is here, on the way to St Eval, down Whitewater.

—*Who wins?*

The one who took en out of the boundary. I picked it up once, coming up the hill, up towards this way, St Columb. The ball went on the ground beside of me. I picked en up and I was out of breath, and then chap from the village come on beside of me, he said, 'Come on Jim.' I was out of breath so I handed en to he. He took en on down to Whitewater. He had – like a feather in your cap.

—*Do people get hurt?*

Not very often. Occasionally somebody take en up and give it a long throw, then people would shout and give 'ee a warning. Course, there's no referee. If I was a little bit irritated with you, I might give you a damn good thump!

Chapel

Chapel life has always been important in the clay villages – as in most of Cornwall. The chapel was a community and arts centre long before such social devices needed to be reinvented. In recent years chapel attendance has declined. Clarence Hancock attended the Greensplat Chapel for most of his life.

I used to love services down there. I used to think that the Methodists in Manchester didn't have much feeling for us small groups down here. Because as the population was going away, we was left with lesser people. And people have changed – a lot of them didn't bother to come, and me and Missus was about the only ones from here, and the children, going down there. We got to such a small crowd then, we couldn't hardly find what they used to call the assessment money. That is, paying to the circuit to find preachers and do all the necessary paperwork. They never spent no money on the chapel. We had to spend our own. The Methodists up in Manchester sent some people along here, to size up the situation as towards the building, what was it like. Well, we had no proper canteen, we had no proper cesspit for our toilets. 'Twas out in the river and went down the pit, and nobody ever bothered about that, over the years, until these blokes come around. Then 'twas totalled up how much it might cost us. We said, 'Oh well, we ain't going to try to get that.' So we jacked it. But we found that, wasn't any good try and keep it going, so eventually it got sold. They sold all the stuff inside, the seats and everything in there.

—Has a decision been made about what will happen to the building?

I don't think there will be a decision made for years now. English China Clay bought it, but since then the French have got it [ECC], ha'n 'em, so what they'll think about Greensplat chapel I don't know. But I think 'tis mostly to stop anybody else coming there. If these works did happen to shut down, somebody could get the idea, 'Oh well, that wouldn't be a bad place to live.'

I was married down there. Children christened down there. I don't think I was ever christened. But I don't think I'm any different about that, because if anybody believe in God, well I do. Couldn't manage without en, could 'ee, when you seriously think about it? How could you manage without God? You couldn't get along very good at all.

The interior of Greensplat chapel, just before the last wedding service – in fact, the last service of any kind – in 1997.

—Do you still manage to go to chapel?

No not now that Missus is in a wheelchair all the time. It's too difficult, and I'm older and weaker.

—You must miss it.

Oh I do. Yes, I used to like going services. We weren't a quiet party. Until the service start, chatter-chatter-chatter. Because we was friendly with everybody, chat with this one, chat with that one. And I used to encourage that sort of thing, because when I was a youngster coming along, my grandfather lived here with us, and he used to go to chapel. And every time he went in through that chapel, he'd say 'Good morning' to somebody on his way up through to his seat. Back in they days they used to have their own seats. He used to have a chat with different ones as he was going up through the chapel, and then as years went on we was even calling each other by their Christian names. We had a lovely friendly bunch and 'twas lovely to go to. Soon as the service start, of course, we were quiet.

Considering the Stars

The religious experience is deep and basic. Les Lean:

I like going up and – always have done – seeing the stars and sky. Last winter when the moon was shining, I say, 'Right, I'm going up now, up top the hill, up Trenance.' I love it up there. See the stars and the moon, and you feel quiet. It feel so still. The first time I felt like that was when I was in my teens. Brother and me went over Summercourt fair – that was about 25 September see, that'd be harvest moon or hunters' moon. We came back, and I was outside our carriage.... Cor, I couldn't believe it, It was beautiful. Lovely. I can understand the chap in the Bible saying, 'When I consider the heavens, the work of thy hands, what is man that thou art mindful of him?' Something marvellous about it all.

CHAPTER 7

Smallholdings and Farm Life

Les Lean and family, outside the railway carriage house. Les is the babe in arms. His father, sitting holding the toddler, is wearing the band medal.

Smallholdings

Where there were clay-works there were smallholdings. Clay-workers and their families were sometimes part-time farmers, sometimes part-time clay-workers, depending on the season and the state of the economy.

I suppose the smallholding was more or less a subsistence operation. That particular farm, I don't know how big it is, but it's like, ten, twelve acres. 'Twas a small farm by local standards, they called it a farm. He would milk

three or four cows and keep pigs and a flock of fowls. The farm still exists. It was a rented farm of course. In local terms he was a farmer. That's what he put on his census returns.

Bob

The Pig Club

The soil in that garden was excellent because, with no running water the toilet was a thunderbox, but with a bucket, and that bucket needed emptying once a week. It was a question of remembering where the last one was buried, and then dig a hole, empty it – splash of Jeyes fluid, and back that would go in the thunderbox. So the garden was well and truly manured. The vegetables were excellent! The other thing that most people did in those days, they kept a shed at the bottom of the garden where they ran a few chickens, so they had fresh eggs. Wherever there was room, they kept a pig which they would perhaps kill once a year. When we had the smallholding we used to keep a couple, but even when we were in the council house we had chicken and a pig, and nearly everyone did the same. [In] the local parish of St Stephen there was a pig club. Everyone who had a pig registered with it, and they would pay sixpence a week. It was like an insurance policy – if for any reason they lost the pig or the pig died, they would be compensated by the pig club. The various districts in the parish had a collector, and they'd have their AGM. The old books of the pig club – there were the names and the families, and for year after year it was the same names, father, son and so on. And then an enquiry if a pig died, whether the compensation was right.

LS

Clay-worker and Farmer

Clarence Hancock remembers his father's smallholding up Greensplat way as a family business.

Biscovillack smallholding – father was running it at the time, working in the clay-pits and running a smallholding just the other side of that house over there, just in the next fields. There was a very old cottage there, and mother and father was in this cottage.

—*How many houses were there in that little bit?*

Just the one. Cow houses and stables for the horses. Because everything was done by horses back then. [Father] used to keep two, one time, for working on the roads. When the Pentewan Road was built his horses was working down there shifting the burden and stuff, as the men were knocking down the banks each side. He had two men driving those horses. At that time he was shaft man, here in the clay-works.

—*How did he combine working in the clay-works and working with his horses?*

Because he had two men to do that. He was employing two men, really. He had acreage enough up there to keep these horses. Back at that time a lot of horses was required to do this sort of work – 'twas done with horse and cart, cutting roads. A lot of work was pick and shovel.

—*How many children were there in the family?*

There was five of us, three girls and two boys. Rhoda was the first, then Violet, then myself, then Walter, and then, several years later Marjory came along. He had a family to keep going as well, so he wanted this money coming in.

—*Did you all have to help on the smallholding?*

Always did, so it come natural. I've built many a hay load, being up top the load, and many hayricks – or helped to build. Stand up on top, and they heave up the hay and then you spread it around to tie it all in. And you had to study the balance of the thing. If your hayrick wasn't sway, like that a bit, then your building wasn't no bloomin' good because eventually he'd go one way and he'd stay there, wouldn't en! You learnt all they dodges, see.

—Did the girls help too?

Oh yes. They used to help mother a lot. But then, hay harvest and corn harvest they was always out doing summat with it. I mean, the girls knew how to rake in straw so that somebody could come along and bind it together. Just pick up some straw and twist it around. put it round the straw, tie a knot, that's that one. For straw, everything had to be put up in shocks. Bundles of straw stand up, so the head of the corn could go on ripening and the water would drain off.

A Helping Hand

Les Lean, same work, same upland area.....

As boys, we used to go up and help Granddad and Uncle carrying hay, summertime. We used to go up on the old horses, building the load. Uncle would say, 'Hold tight!' That horse be gone, like. You had to make sure you catch hold of the horse, just put up a hand, hold tight, because the horse would know what he's saying, start going on. I was helping Uncle up on Greensplat right up until recently, with bales of hay. Now, they got big round ones, but when they had the bales of hay, Uncle'd ring up, 'Oh Les, I'm carrying hay....' And I used to go up there all the time and help him.

—I think everybody used to help everybody else, didn't they. Did the women help each other out?

No, no, no. You never used to see much woman at all; used to be indoors. On a smallholding they'd do little jobs when they had to, like out building the rick, helping out when 'tis haytime, when 'tis busy. They used to bring out the drinks. We used to have herby beer. Know what herby beer is? Made with herbs. Taste lovely when you'm sweating and hot, herby beer.

—Is that alcoholic?

No. I shouldn't think so, because we was all Methodist [laughs]. We had to take the pledge up Sunday School every year. They would read out all the names of the Sunday School, you had to say that you'd kept the

Les outside the door of the railway carriage house.

vow. Your name... yes, yes. You didn't break the vow, you didn't have any drink. Men as well. Grown-ups as well. I've never had a pint of beer in my life, not even now.

—*Was all your family teetotal?*

That's right. No smokers nor nothing.

The Housewife

Smallholding had its downside, especially if you were a busy housewife like Phyllis Webber.

I used to work from eight till five. Run the home, washing, ironing, cooking. I used to do a lot of baking then. That was working and looking after the poultry. It was all right during the summer, but in the winter months – you get the wind howling and the rain, and it was freezing cold. And then you got to go round to feed up, and you go to shut in, and you get an awkward one that won't go in. You say, 'Oh my goodness, who'd be out tonight! I want to get in, I want to get in!' And there I am, dripping and cold. Geese are lovely, ducks are beautiful but chicken, they're so stupid.

One goose once – we had a beautiful grey goose and she was broody and I couldn't get her off this nest. I tried all sorts of things and I thought, Oh its no good, I can't, I can't. So I meant to have left a note for John to say about it and forgot all about it, hoping and praying that she was there the next morning. Oh no. Freddy Fox had been round. That's nothing to what he did to that new [chicken] house with all those cockerels in. He ripped all the back of the shed off, so don't people talk to me about fox. Oh he did do some damage. He ripped, broke it, and got in and killed all the cockerels, and they were all fattening up ready for Christmas. Beauties they were. About a dozen in there. He took one and left the others all dead on the floor. John said, 'That's a fox.' And that's when I was educated.

Farms and Farm Workers

David Field came originally from up-country. He vividly remembers his first day at the Cornish farm where he was to spend the rest of his working life.

When I got to the station there was no transport. There was a local town bus that used to service a lot of the trains, but the day that I came down the people at Teagles Farm had all gone off to the Royal Cornwall. I arrived in the middle of the afternoon and because there was no one there to pick me up, I said [to the stationmaster] 'Well how far is it?' He said, 'It's not all that far, it's about four miles,' – so I decided to walk. As I walked it became more and more interesting. I can remember stopping at Tregaswith, and there was this very old man (to me). I expect he was about sixty; rather bluff, quite large, he had quite a large corporation. He sort of stuck his fingers in his belt and talked to me. He gave me directions to the farm. He was working in the doorway of a barn, and I remember looking into this barn and seeing these barrels in the background. I said, 'You make cider then. What do you keep in your barrels?' 'Oh no,' he said, 'those barrels came ashore in Mawgan Porth at the end of the war. They were full of wine. We rescued them.' At the time it sounded very attractive and very colourful, but I've heard since that the wine wasn't particularly good quality and that you had to be pretty hard-headed to drink any of it.

David (on the left), harvesting with his youngest son in 1985.

I walked further on to the farm, which is in an attractive position with rather an attractive house and garden. When I got there, there was a cousin looking after the place, a girl. I suppose she was about sixteen, seventeen. She'd been asked to go over to keep an eye on the place whilst they were away at the show. She said, 'They won't be back till about six. I'll give you some tea'. I said, 'It's a bit early for that, can I go and have a look round?' There was a public road which ran up through the farm, and she said, 'The farm lies on either side of the road.' I walked up the road about a mile, and when I got to the top of the farm there was quite a big field, about thirty acres, and not far off the road there was this little wooden radar station, with a wooden mast at the top. I went over and had a look at it. It was obviously abandoned, and they'd been using it to store hay in. I climbed up the little mast at the top – there was a sort of

David Field at Trevithick Farm, 1950.

Jim Ellery at the Talskiddy village pump in the 1970s.

ladder going up the side, and there was a ladder going up the mast which gave you about another 30 feet of panoramic view. I remember looking round, and you could see the whole of the valley. You could see over the St Mawgan aerodrome and over the neighbouring farm and towards Newquay – it was a very attractive view. I can remember being so impressed with this I thought, I must come back again, I'd love to come back again. This was before I'd met any of the family, before I knew anything about what the job was or what the background was. But I can remember this feeling of great attraction towards it, which has lasted. I'm still here.

—Coming as you did from up-country, did you find it difficult to get accepted by the older farmworkers on this Cornish farm?

I started when there was so much more hand labour, when every sheaf was pitched, you pitched your sheaves onto a wagon, and you subsequently unloaded the wagon and pitched them up into the shed or into a rick. I helped build ricks. I was quite good at building ricks. A lot of the farm workers didn't like being up on ricks, they didn't want the responsibility of building them. A lot of people seem to get cramp if they're on very soft... this is one of the things they said, 'If I get up on the rick for too long, if I'm up there all day, I come off with a terrible cramp in my legs.' That never worried me. I'd always been a rick man and the rick man is always slightly above, in status, from the man who's pitching it onto the rick. He always gets more respect than the others. If the rick falls over or loses shape, as ricks can so easily do, then you get all the flak, but if you build a good rick.... If you're not afraid to pitch in with the others then they accept you, you're one of they.

Rabbits Everywhere

Back along, before myxomatosis, rabbits proliferated on all farmland. Jim Ellery again:

My father always kept a pony or a couple of cobs. He was a trapper, that's how he got his money. I got the book here now of what he give – down on Bedruthan and out St Enoder. It was better for trapping out there, they kept their hedges up. But here, some places the blinking hedges was all gone down. The rabbits was coming out from anywhere, it was like a beehive. I said to my father one time down Denzell, I got up on the old hedge, I sunk down – I said, 'The old hedges here are hollow.' 'No,' he said, 'they will be – but they'm full of rabbits now!'

—How did you catch em, did you have a gun?

Never fired a gun in my life, nor my father. Gins. Not allowed to, now. We didn't realize.... I put my hand in one once to see what 'twas like. Just like a door come home on your fingers. Poor old rabbit got frightened more than anything. You don't really realize. Children can be – what's the big word, fine word – oblivious.

—So you've caught your rabbits. Then what?

Opened em, took out their pots. We call 'em pots. Their guts, punch. Punch the rabbits. Why they call it punch, I don't know, and my father used to send them away one time....

    To eat too much we know is wrong;
    Come children let us now discourse
      Upon the faithful useful horse.
     On his back men ride with ease;
    He carries them just where they please.
      Along the road or up the hill,
     Though there his task is harder still,
     And if to make more haste they need,
      He'll gallop with the greatest speed.
That's it.

They memorized it by rhymes. A lot of people couldn't read then. I knew a couple in the village, they weren't deficient up here but they couldn't read. They hadn't had schooling. My father – very slow reader. If he see a thing in the paper he'd ask you to read it, although he had fellers employed. But he knew his onions.

CHAPTER 8

The Land

Dorienne Robinson.

Conservation

When the clay companies were kings, the land was there to be used, not looked at. But now there is much derelict land. Stagnant pools of green water and waste-mounds of various shapes and sizes. Questions are being asked. Shouldn't the clay industry start cleaning up after itself? Can the land ever return to its original moorland/downland state? An opinion from Dorienne Robinson, a local Green Party member.

Once the pits become disused and start to revert back to nature, they become the most wonderful wildlife sites. They're incredibly rich with birds, insects, birds of prey, badgers, foxes – all those sorts of things that just move in. Once the site's been worked out, and it's just left as a hole in the ground and reverts, nobody goes there for anything, there's no need. It just goes back to being quiet, goes back to being peaceful. Nobody disturbs it, and of course, in they all come, into the pits they go. A lot of the old tin mines are wonderful habitats for bats. There is a case for old industrial landscapes to be left just as they are, they do make wonderful nature reserves. It'll all come creeping back in. Purple loosestrife, and then the insects and everything else, and you'll suddenly find it's a very rich habitat.

Dust from the Tips

Joan Vincent campaigned tirelessly for many years.

I used to talk about the dust, the noise, the loss of sunlight – in the morning at dawn, and also in the evening when it was setting. There was quite a difference, with all the massive hills. The County Council never ever believed me until I told them to go to a certain position, and have a look at the sunlight going down. Then they could see what I was talking about.

—Was that in this area?

Yes. The Caerloggas Downs was one. If you went to Penwithick you'd have the sun setting about forty minutes earlier, purely through that tip. And the dust – I can well remember, it was a weekend in May. I don't know how many years ago that was, but we had a very dry spell and then we had the easterly wind that suddenly got up one day. We were completely obliterated with the dust and the gravel blowing down from the

Joan Vincent, 1999.

Caerloggas tip. Doris Ansari was chairman of planning at that time so I drove down to Truro and got her, brought her up to show her what was happening. I've never seen anything like it. Everything in the gardens, even half a mile away, was completely covered with white; the fishpond was covered with white – my goldfish died. You couldn't open your eyes, you couldn't open your mouth, because it was just blowing. People had accepted it in the past, because they said Well, you can't do anything against English China Clays. And I said, Well you can. You've got to stand up and fight, which is what I did.

The problems that we had, that I exposed, and had been all kept quiet – properties were being tipped right close to,

A clay-tip encroaching on housing at Foxhole; the date is unknown.

right to the bottom of their garden, and then they would just offer them the current market value – with a tip at the bottom of their garden – they were almost worthless. I did get a letter out of them saying that they would pay the full market price. But they used to object to even people building a bathroom or a lavatory, or anything.

—*English China Clays objected?*

Yes. that's right.

—*As if they were a local authority!*

Yes. It was quite amazing. Quite amazing, the power that they had – purely over that local plan.

—*How did the local people react to your campaigning?*

The older generation would never criticize English China Clays, because, they said, they've been our bread and butter. They've provided us with jobs and we are quite happy with the way that things are. The middle generation, forties, fifties group, were beginning to question, but I think that I made them aware of what was going on. I don't think that they could see the extent of what was actually going on – they couldn't see what was going to happen in the future. The younger generation were very different. The younger generation said, We are not going to tolerate this. We don't want this mess that we've been landed with.

—*Now that Caerloggas Down has been reprofiled and restored, how is it shaping up?*

It's wonderful. Heather's regenerating, the skylarks are back. It was a wonderful place before. We used to walk there as children. You'd find skylarks' nests everywhere up there. There was a lot of footpaths. We did lose all the footpaths across there. Back then it was heather, what we call urts, whortleberries, masses and masses of those up there, and I've said I would like to see that reintroduced, if we can.

Years ago when I was a child [the clay country] was a very beautiful area. It was full of heather, moorland, and very attractive, with the little conical tips. Now, in my opinion, the countryside has been raped and left with devastation, like a lunar landscape. And that's what I'm trying to put right.

Rebirth of a Valley

On the western edge of the clay country, Babs Bennett has discovered a neglected valley.

[Tregargus valley] was a series of china stone mills powered by water. They crushed stone. They started in about the 1870s and finished about 100 years later when the market collapsed. It's a steep sided valley, but you can still feel a pulse there. Its most – I was going to say eerie, it's not eerie, it's a very friendly – it's like someone who's asleep. That's why I call it the sleeping valley. It's asleep. It needs to be reborn, a bit like the princess. We have to – not put ourselves on the map for posterity and national reasons, but for the well being, psychologically, of the people who live here. They have something of worth here, which is worth cherishing and handing on. The fact that it's of national importance is a by-product.

It must have been a hive of activity. I mean, one mill on top of another, going up this valley. I think some of the central ones now

Joan Vincent being made a Cornish bard (with singer Joseph Luxon), 1992.

Babs Bennett.

A decaying industrial site in Tregargus valley.

Peace in Tregargus valley, October 1999.

are no more – they've been demolished. I walked part of it a year ago last September. It's just overgrown, you can't see a lot because nature has taken over, but there is this little tiny granite building with no roof, no door, no window in it, and beside it the relic of a water wheel, iron water wheel. There's another [building] with a little cottage beside it. The leafmould must be nearly 18 inches thick on the floor. You can hear the birds, you can hear the river whispering through. It's a very peaceful, a very calm, very comforting feeling.

Landscape

The landscape around the lost village of Karslake was an odd mixture of industrial wasteland and the original moorland. Clayton Roberts:

It was completely open moorland, heather and gorse, with the occasional tip.

—Like Bodmin Moor?

Yes, very similar sort of terrain. You had a sand road going into the houses – which they did tarmac part way after a while, but the rest of it was sand road, and then you got to this hamlet and that was it. The rest was downs. They parked these houses in the middle of the downs.

—Did those houses have gardens?

They had gardens. I can't remember anybody ever growing anything up there. All I can remember of the gardens, it was all wild. I think there might have been people

104

who done their garden but I can't remember seeing any bean rows. I think there might have been potatoes grown up there.

—Were there trees?

No. No trees. When you used to drive along the road to get to Karslake you could see the pit slowly open up, and it looked like these houses were precariously balanced on the side of this pit. [The pit edge] slowly came back over the years, so when I left you could literally go down the bottom of the garden and then about twenty or thirty yards you could walk along and it just disappeared into the pit.

People made the landscape, and gave their names to their creations.

The pits was named after families. Down at Quarry Close there was a pit called 'T's', and that was a man called T. Stevens. Another quarry was called 'Allen's'. These men used to be bookies in the quarries – that's the charge-hands. There was another pit – I can't never remember that working – called 'Cathedral', and that stone was taken from there down to Truro cathedral. There was another quarry called 'Purple' because it used to produce hard purple stone. And families would go in generations. In this yer T's family, I can remember three generation in that quarry. There was another quarry called Brewers quarry. A man called Fred Brewer used to... and that name always stuck there.

Goss Moor

One area remains almost untouched by recent industrial working – though even Goss Moor was half created by the old tin streamers. It is

A clay landscape: rosebay willowherb, fields and a decaying tip.

Goss Moor is the scrubland in the foreground. In the middle ground is rough grazing reclaimed from the moor, and the line of the A30. [EN]

now threatened not by the clay industry, but by the motor car. Widening of the A30 to take more cars faster to somewhere is probably going to take place. Susan Taylor lives near and works on the Moor.

It's what you call a low-profile reserve. It's not one of these aesthetically pleasing ones, like the Lizard. To people round here it's just Goss Moor, what we've always been used to. If you live next door to something you don't think it's anything special. If you were a butterfly person or a dragonfly person, you'd say, 'Oh yes, it's very good down there.'

A lot of people take their dogs down, and more and more people are walking down there now. The kids have been down, and they've gone home and told the parents – we always give them a leaflet now when they come down. They know it's accessible. We only marked out the access tracks about two or three years ago. A lot of it's inaccessible because of the type of ground. It's so wet you've got to stay on the path. From a conservation point of view it's great, because people don't go in off the path, because if you do you can get lost – literally – and never be found again. It's a boggy mire. There's a peat base on a lot of it. You can stand on it, it'll move like a carpet. You can walk across some of it now, but give it six months and you wouldn't be able to walk across it anywhere. It'd be too wet. You'd be up to your thighs in water. The locals use the paths because they know where they are, but that's only the main tracks. Only a fool goes off.

—You and your husband have turned conservation into a small business. I suppose some of your customers have a misguidedly romantic attitude to the countryside and conservation?

People have gone and bought four or five acres, and you go past it and you think... ohhh! Or, 'I've got a couple of acres I want cut'. 'Yes, well what are you doing with it?' 'Oh, nothing; it's my nature area.' And all it is, is grass. There's nothing else in it, no diversity, nothing. They can't do nothing with it because it's got too long, no advantage whatsoever. Or they've had one pig, one cow, one goat; one of everything and they just don't understand what they're doing. Or they've got hundreds of trees planted in one little space. 'They're not doing very well, I don't understand it,' – and you've got to try and explain, as

nicely as possible, that it may be better to do it like this – you have actually got to cut round that. Nature doesn't work on its own. You've got to work at it to produce what you want. It's like with the heathland, you've got to manage it. It evolves. You have grassland, then you have scrubland, and then you have woodland. That woodland'll gradually crash down and then you'll start again. They don't see it. They see an end result but they don't see the 150 years before it, to get to the high forest stage. A hundred years ago you'd have a woodsman in every wood. There'd be somebody in picking up dead wood, coppicing, pollarding; all that would be done. People would have the right to go in [the wood] and take this and take that, and do the work. But nobody does it now. Somebody's got to be paid to go in and do it.

Roadside wild flowers near Greensplat, June 1999.

A blocked path.

Paths

Many of the old clay-workers' trails are now closed or have disappeared.

Up top the hill you mean. There was a path. Now – I was looking the other day, they stopped that. They got a sign up there – This isn't a through road, it's a cul-de-sac. I expect they want to tip something or do something down the bottom. Well, 'tis all wrong really. That should have gone right down through.

—Because you used to use it?

Yep.

LL

Peter Bishop, of the Ramblers' Association, works hard to keep paths open – and has useful information on how to survive in farming country.

There's five [Ramblers'] groups in the county, and each group has its own right of way officer. I'm right of way officer for Restormel. Last year I had the parish of St Gorran. We walked every single footpath in the parish. It took us three or four months – we did it weekends, evenings and so on, and before the county had a chance to fix it, the parish council went out and fixed every blooming thing in sight. They're a very conscientious council.

—When you start on a new parish, what state are the paths usually in?

In some parishes they'll be so neglected it'll be terrible. In others they'll be almost perfect. Some years ago we did this exercise for the Ordnance Survey. I had a 2-kilometre square, down on the way to Truro. I had seven footpaths on my patch. Five were totally blocked, one was partially blocked and one was very difficult to find because it wasn't signposted.

—Do some farmers object to your presence on their land?

Oh yes. One we had not far from here. I wasn't quite sure where the footpath ran. I went over and saw the farmer and said, 'Could you possibly tell me where the footpath runs?' I came out of the farmyard and there was a shotgun under my dog's ear, and he walked me off with a shotgun. He was very lucky I didn't go to the police and get a criminal charge against him. It took us three years, but at the end of three years he had to stand there, and [he] said, 'The footpath goes across that field – and mind my bloody potatoes!' He eventually sold the farm and left.

I've got some old maps [of the clay area] which show footpaths going here, there and everywhere. Look at a modern one and it's just a big white splodge because the whole lot is now a clay-pit. You hear people say, 'I want to walk that way' – but they can't. This is an industrial landscape, and a lot of these paths were there – people just wandered across them, the workers. That was land owned by their employers, and they walked across the land to get home. By implication, they were using that land with permission of the employer. That's a special case. It

Narrow road, steep incline, blind corner, heavy lorry. This is Greensplat – but it could be practically anywhere in the clay country.

doesn't mean that the general public has the right to do so. One's got to say that ECCI are very generous. They've taken areas which they've stopped working and they've helped set up footpaths – out of their own pockets – set it up and said, 'Right, there's an amenity for the general public.'

A lot of the roads here are very narrow. They were never designed to take the traffic we have now. We're very different from a lot of other places in that we have very high hedgerows – they're an extension of the old green lanes – so we can't expand the roads, it's a major undertaking. And a lot of our roads are absolutely minute. In some places, literally touching the sides of the roads as you go along. I took a friend of mine – who came across from America – I took him down Hemmick, down on the coast, a beautiful little beach, but the road going down it is ...the car touches as you go down, and it winds in and out. There's hardly any passing places so it's quite chaotic – and it's not a one way system either. I took him down there, and all I could hear was him going, 'Oh my god, oh my god, oh my god.'

—*I believe cattle can be quite dangerous to walkers.*

People think, 'Bull' – that can be quite dangerous. It's not the bulls that are dangerous, it's the cows. Young steers, I think, are the worst of the lot because young steers are very excitable. You go in – especially if you've got a dog with you – they come and have a sniff, and then they jump about. When they're jumping about, they don't mean to hurt you but – you get in the way of half a ton of cow who's leaping about and throwing his feet in the air (as they quite often do) it can be very nasty. If you've got cows in a field with young calves you've got to be wary of them.

—*Is there a way of avoiding trouble?*

I've never had any trouble with them. If it's young heifers I tend to walk straight at them. I don't let them crowd into me. I keep the dog under close control. If I had to, I'd leave her go, because she's OK, she can run faster than they can. She's terrified of them anyway. If you can, you walk around, but if they start coming back at you, you go for them. You never run away from them. You never walk away from them, because if you walk away they're following you. They'll come after you and suddenly they'll start galloping and jumping about and kicking their feet in the air. But if you crowd into them, you'll push them back all the time. If it's a cow with a young calf and she's being protective, I would walk round her. You don't get aggressive to her, you don't try and push her back, because you won't.

—*Many footpaths go through farmyards. Have you ever had trouble with farm dogs?*

Farm dogs are a pest, some of them. I've got my own technique to deal with them. If one's coming right at me I just stand there and I throw my arms out, point at it and yell at it. Yaaa! And they go – Prrrk! I've never had one attack me yet.

CHAPTER 9

Clay Country Characters

A later assembly of clay-work characters, in 1984. Clayton Roberts is second on the left.

Laying Out the Dead

Bob's mother was a woman to be reckoned with.

Mother's brag was, she had a face like a gaol door. [Laughs] Proud of it. Actually she was a very good looking woman. She could face anybody out. Mother shaved her first corpse by the time she was fifteen.

—Was that part of the job?

Oh yes. Everybody was put in their best and shaved and titched up to go in the box. If anybody died the undertaker would want the barber to come and shave them – especially if they'd been ill for a while. There might have been two or three days' growth on them, mightn't there? And all the people that were in bed and too ill to shave – she would have a note come, 'Will you visit so-and-so tonight and shave him?' She would kneel on his chest, legs either side, and lather him up, shave him in bed.

Her training bore good fruit.

Mother had the right idea really. Once I'd decided to go to Camborne School of Mines I then knew, if I was going abroad, I was carrying Piran's flag. I had to be... not fall down on the job. I went in training for it in my own – training myself. I did silly things when I was a teenager, sixteen, seventeen. I used to go out for a long walk and make sure that I walked through Stenalees cemetery during the course of the walk. The first few times I wasn't happy doing it but in the end you go through just like you go through any field. Walk in one gate and out the other. I wasn't very happy with heights, so I found a place where an old pipe track – a six-inch pipe had been laid on the ground and the sand from the burrow had washed out over it, so it appeared to come out from underground. I used to walk along that one pipe and drop off. Well, of course he's lying on the ground. And then two pipes and drop off. A little further on 'twas about 18 inches up. And then it was up on a horse [a supporting frame] and eventually it crossed an old small pit with a few inches of water and some clay in the bottom, and with trees growing, perhaps 25, 30ft up. I walked out a little further each day, and turn around and come back until I could walk right across the deep place. 'Twasn't long before I used to come home, throw my satchel down, run over the road, down the lane, over that pipe, up the other lane and home, whether it was rain or shine, just to beat that phobia. Now, there was a time or two in Africa when I was glad of that.

The Pump House

An encounter with an old clay-worker, who impressed Clayton Roberts.

When I first went down to the pump-house – I think I had to do a month training in this pump-house – twenty minutes would have cracked it but you got to do a month – the first day I went down there, there's this old boy in there smoking a pipe. He said, 'You right then boy?' Puff-puff-puff-puff. I said, 'All right, mate, yeah. Not bad.' 'Who are you then?' I told him who I was. He said, 'Oh yeah, you'm Clar's boy, yeah yeah.' Puff-puff-puff. – and he's smoking this pipe. He said, 'Well yer 'tiz. There it is, boy.' I said, 'Oh, right.'

And there's this room, about 20-odd foot by 12, and you got this bloody great pump in there, you know – chug-chug-chug-chug-chug – massive pump, 6, 7ft high. In some of the newer places, later on, they actually built a little sectioned off, double-glazed piece, so you never had to be in the room with the heat and the dirt and the noise, but at that time you actually stood in there. And if you looked down you could see the wear on the floorboards, the years of walking up and down by the window and over by the winch. It was all manual. As things developed later on, in some of the places you had electric winches to winch the suction pipe up and down, but this was all done manually then, and you could see the wear on the floorboards, over the years, where people had marched.

I said, 'How long have you been down here then, mate?' 'Oooh,' he said, 'ever since I was a youngster,' he said. 'Fifteen.' And he was coming up to retirement. He said, 'No, tell a lie,' he said, 'I did have six years off for the war.'

That was the only time he'd ever spent out of that pump house, and he had to go and fight a bloody war to get out of it. So he'd been there for forty-odd years. Oh my god. he's been here, in this spot, for all this time. He's contributed to making this trench in the floor. His pipe went out, so he knocked his pipe out, put it on the window ledge – and we're looking out at the pool – he took out Robin Redbreast pipe tobacco. He undone the wrapping and he put the wrapping in his tin and threw the tobacco out the window.

I said, 'Here mate, You just chucked your baccy out the window.' He said, 'Aw, bugger me,' he said, 'so I have.' We're down there now with bit of stick, trying to get this tobacco out the water – anyway, it was no go. I said, 'Ah, for goodness sake!' He said, 'Oh bugger and hell,' he said, 'I got no bloody baccy now for the shift.' Well, I used to smoke ordinary tailor-made fags then. I said, 'Have a fag.' He said, 'I can't smoke they. I'll tell 'ee what, I'll break one up and put en in me pipe.'

So for the rest of the day he was breaking up cigarettes and putting them in his pipe. Of course it was...tff-tff, tff-tff...because it was very finely cut, and he was spitting. .... I believe I'm right in saying that this particular guy has died. Coming out of the pit, he had a heart attack. The problem is, you're so inactive in the job, you get very, very unfit and the only exercise you've got is walking out the pit. Now, you've got eight hours of doing bugger-all, and then all of a sudden, ten minutes of acute exertion walking out of this pit, hundreds of steps. And of course he smoked like a train. Boredom. Smoke and eat, that's all you can do down there. Or read a book. I got into reading in quite a big way.

At the end of my time with ECCI, I was myself in a pump-house up at Penhale pit, and I went down there one morning shift, tired and fed up with it, and I was smoking roll-ups. I took the paper off my tobacco, I put the paper in my tin and I threw the tobacco out the window....and it horrified me. I thought, my god, I've just done what matey had done twelve years previous. And that was the day I decided to leave. I thought, I've got to get out of it.

Modern Clay-work

In spite of modern developments, clay-work can still be fun – and dangerous. John Cloke:

I suppose I've always been a diesel cowboy, I've always been a bit of a rebel. I like that type of life. We're professionals, and if you're not happy in it you wouldn't do it. If you see fear in it, you wouldn't do it. I've been in situations where it's been scary. I knew if I'd got out of that machine I would never drive no more.

—What sort of situations?

Side of the face has given way. Like in the picture [a photograph John was showing me] where the dumper's upside down. If I thought that would happen again I would never have drove no more. But I got right back in and carried on – I had to. I turned, she wouldn't go around and as I turned I knew he was going to go over. There was no way he was going to stay on the road, so as I went around the bend I knew exactly where he was going to go. I thought to myself, 'Oh shit.' I dived across the cab and just prayed. I didn't remember him going over. I felt him beginning to rock and sway a bit. Next thing

John Cloke's dumper truck and a car – hopefully not the boss's!

I knowed, I was climbing out the door. A couple of the blokes was there by this time, stopped. Helped me down off the wheel. I was shaking but I knew what had happened. I got in another dumper and carried on driving.

Pit Accidents

George Morcom, a clay country character talking about clay country characters.
—There must have been a few accidents in the pits?

Oh yes. After the war – there wasn't a lot of regulations, about places of safety to go [during blasting]. There was a place in the pit a long way back where they had a canteen, and it had a concrete roof. All the men were supposed to go back there and when they were blasting some of them wouldn't do that. They would go part way back – as long as they could get theirself under cover. There was one chap there – him and another chap was on the hose. He had a very pronounced humped back, and he was wearing two oilers at the time, one outside the other, because the oilers weren't all that good. [The two of them] retreated as far as they thought they was safe and there was a jubilee wagon stuck up on its end there, and they stick their heads in there with their asses sticking out. When it went off, this stone hit him – just on the back. He was in agonies. I knew a bit about first aid and I couldn't touch him, he was in such agonies. I couldn't undress him or do anything with him. I come to the conclusion he'd broke his pelvis because he couldn't stand or anything. I got two long splints and tied his legs, feet and knees

Meledor Clay Works tug-o'-war team, 1938. George Morcom is second from the left on the front row.

together, as you would do it for a pelvis injury – extended from under the armpits right down; tied him up best way I could and got him on a stretcher. You couldn't get down into the pits at that time, but we had an incline there which wasn't all that stiff and men started carrying him out.

Well, the best way he could lie was a bit sideways on the stretcher. His back, with a slight hump in it normally, was showing a lot more than what it should be, and one bloke come on, he said, 'My God, he's broke his back'. Anyhow, we got him to the top. Someone said, 'You ought to go over and tell his wife' – he lived close by. He said, 'Don't tell my wife. Only last night she said, "You wash your feet; what if you're hurt tomorrow".' He was home the next day. He had bad bruises for a few days, but he hadn't broke no bones. I suppose the fact that he

George Morcom, 1999.

Tom Browne, in his prime.

Tom Browne in 1999.

had two oilers on must have cushioned the blow but the stone that hit him was quite big, about six or seven pound, which is like a cannon ball coming down, isn't it.

A Fight to be Proud of

Tom Browne, the St Blazey athlete, found himself in Australia during the Second World War. This is the only fight which he remains proud of.

This old chap, he was an old man and his wife was a very old lady in her eighties. There was a big grocery shop there and a fruiterer's place and I got talking – the one that owned the shop, he was in there and a jolly old chap he was, and he came from Tregony, down here. When I told him I was down St Blazey, 'Hell', he said, 'I heard of that place, it's not far away'. I said, 'No, 'tisn't far away.'

Couple of days later this old man said, 'Come on, I'll show 'ee another little pub down in Therrule' – well, there was only two there. 'Ess, I don't mind.' We went down there and had a yarn and laugh and that. It's closing at six o'clock in they days when the war was on so, 'Come on then boy,' he said, 'we'll walk across the road, we'll catch a bus home.' We walked across the road together, and there was three Australian soldiers there, and all three of 'em had their legs in irons. So I walked over. I said, 'Where'd 'ee catch that bloody lot then?' 'Oh, up in the islands, with the Japs. They had a machine gun there and lucky – all three of us lived.'

The old man said, 'Oh my Christ!' I said, 'What's the matter with you?' 'Over across the other side of the road.' So I looked, and there was these four men there. I said, 'What about they?' 'Oh, they'm the bloody terrors of the little village here, bullies.' 'Oh', I said, 'here we go.' I knew right away.

These four started shouting at these soldiers, and that made me worse than ever. They couldn't defend theirselves or do nothing. Lucky to have any life at all, really. The old man said, 'I know 'em; don't bloody well say anything. Let them go'. One of them happened to spot that I was a British sailor, so now I started getting it from them, the abuse.

I took off my hat. I said, 'Here hold my hat.' I can see it now as if 'twas yesterday. He said, 'For Christ... don't', he said, 'they'll kill ya.' I said, 'You wait and see.' Well, to cut the story short, I laid the bloody four of em out – and really laid 'em out. I didn't pull no punches – half their teeth out. I come other side the road [to] these soldiers, I said, 'You're all right now.' 'Yes,' he said, 'that was bloody brilliant,' he said. I said, 'I was mad.' I was, with temper.

Tom also had his softer side.
—*What made you join the church choir?*

My mother took me to Sunday school when I was four, and I stayed with them until I was fifteen. I became an altar boy as well. I wish I could sing like it now. I'd sing to you.

—*What's your favourite hymn?*

Well, I love 'em all really, more than I do songs. But – 'Immortal, invisible, God only wise'. Do you know it? Can 'ee sing it? [Tom sings. I mutter along.]

I had a good voice back along. Sometimes he'll come back, you know. Sunday nights [in the pub] that's all we would sing, is hymns. We'd come back along...all the cottages is gone. We used to be going along from Pack Horse [pub] and we'd say, 'Hang on, stop. We'll have this one here.' And they all used to open their windows. We'd be singing. 'Give us another one, give us another one,' the older people would say. We'd sing a few more and then go on. 'Hang on, sing this one a minute'. I used to go off singing carols, make some money. Yes, done well on that.

Church Rivalry

A good tale from just outside clay country. Mrs Blanche Williams, interviewed by Joy Payne, throws light on religious attitudes in mid-Cornwall earlier last century.

I was playing the organ in St Eval church. Well I went this chapel with my sister-in-law. We rode our bicycles to chapel, went in, the Sunday afternoon. My cousin – she died and the daughter, she come to me and she said, 'You play', she said. 'I don't feel like playing because mother used to play here and she's only now buried.' So I said, 'Oh no, I don't mind a bit.' Well in the evening – 'twas a funny thing to do I suppose – I went to the church, and it was the Revd Johnson was the preacher there. Well he was very high church, you see.

Course I walked in the vestry and I said, 'Well, have you made out the evening hymns?' – because I used to put them on the board. He said, 'I've got something I want to say to you.' I said, 'Yes?'- thinking 'twas something about playing. So he said, 'I hear you've been to the Methodist chapel this

Blanche Williams with her husband and son, Tony, in 1937.

Blanche Williams in the 1980s.

afternoon – and done worse than that. You've played the organ there.' Somebody, see, told him in that few hours. He said, 'We're not having that. You're playing this one' – and he tapped our organ – we were in the vestry – 'or,' he said, 'you go there'.

I said, 'I shall go there, because my cousin has died, and the daughter said would I do it for four weeks as a favour. I can see no wrong in that.' He said, 'What about the choir? There's thirty-two here in the choir.'

'Well,' I said, 'it's your doing. You've told me I must do one or the other. I've made my choice.'

—What happened in the end?

I done the both.

CHAPTER 10

Agriculture

Frank Davey on his Fordson tractor.

Diversification

Farming and clayworking are intertwined, both in space and time. Both have changed the landscape. Both have had to change with the times, and with advancing technology. Frank Davey:

There was a time when the Ministry of Agriculture gave a grant to farmers to make

their fields bigger, but when the average acreage of the fields on our farm got to about sixteen to twenty acres, then I felt enough was enough; that was big enough. But prior to that we had fields of six acres and five acres and ten acres – for modern machinery it was so inefficient.

—Your farm, the one you were brought up on, is that still going strong?

Old sheds on Walter Bloomfield's farm in a remote part of central Cornwall.

Oh yes, yes. We decided to move into the tourism business as one diversification that we could have on the farm and we opened the farm to the public. They could come into the farmyard and see the milking being done every day. Coupled with this my brother has, over his lifetime, collected a lot of Victorian machinery and farming artefacts, so we had something to show them. We could put a little price tag on it, which gave us another source of income, and this worked very well. It was highly successful for ten years, until a lot of other people could see.....and were encouraged also by the government to have diversifications on their farm. Some of them took in bed and breakfast, some decided to have pony trekking, some made golf courses on their farm.

Bad Times

There were bad times in the thirties, there are bad times now. Walter Bloomfield's story could have happened in either period.

And since then it's gone back the same trend now. Calves, they're some cheap really. They're selling for about a pound, two pound each, and all. Well there's a feller that went to Helston market with his van, and he wanted a calf. All right, he bought the calf, put it in the van, loaded it up, that was all right. Well he never thought no more of that. Then when he got home there was two calves in there. Somebody give en one calf, because they wasn't making anything and they was losing money. You aren't earning nothing really. You have a calf, you take it to market, sell it and all. Well all as you have is about a quid or two pound, and the bloody lorry man got to be paid, the auctioneer got to be paid, so the feller's losing money.

—*Were you sad when you had to sell the farm?*

Not at all. I wasn't able to do it. If you was able to do it, I wouldn't mind to have done it. Well now that I wasn't able to do it I don't want to do it. You just can't. That's your lot, mister, time is catching up [laughs]. [Farming] is a hell of a job. I don't know as I would like to go back to it again. You can't miss a day of it out. That's no good, 'tis a full-time job.

Overgrown and Derelict

Herbicide spraying – the how and the why. Richard Dudden explains:

I was looking for a farm that no one else really wanted, a neglected farm – without being disrespectful to whoever the previous owner may have been – a neglected farm that I could turn into money. Overgrown hedges, derelict buildings. It satisfied the previous owner. He made his living, he was happy there. But I thought, 'Here's a challenge, here's a way to make a pound.' I had to put a lot of money into it of course. A lot of money. I poured a lot of money into that farm, but it paid its reward.

A lot of the fields were absolutely riddled with couch [grass]. We did a blanket spray and killed it all. Give you an idea of how poor [the land] was, one field we ploughed and planted with winter barley. It was a twenty-acre field, but the overgrowth of the hedges was so great, and undrained land, blocked up land-drains, we only planted

Richard Dudden at a ploughing match, 1948.

Threshing, old style. Richard (right) and his father are on top of the drum in 1956.

thirteen acres of it. The rest was overgrown. We had ten tons of grain off it. So that shows how poor the land was. We laid it down to grass and got the boundaries right back to their original positions, drained the wet patches, and then ploughed it all up again and planted it to winter wheat. So that was twenty acres. We had three tons to the acre off, first crop.

Nearly every field was – the hedge boundaries were grossly overgrown and we carved them off with a power saw on a hedge trimmer, and pushed it up into heaps with an old JCB that we had; burnt it, and cut back to the original-sized fields. You can't farm in a jungle. We pushed it up into great big heaps – that was prior to planting the fields – planted the corn round the heaps of stick. We couldn't burn them because the birds nested in the heaps of stick, so we had

to wait to the autumn when the birds finished nesting before we could burn the stick.

—Is that a rule or was that your choice?

No, choice. Didn't want to destroy nature; that would be cruel. We knew the birds were nesting there, all sorts, types of birds. And they were big heaps of timber, not wood. They burnt right to the ashes, and all we had to do was spread the ashes on the land. And the land appreciated the ashes we gave it.

—How did you get rid of the couch grass?

Spraying with Roundup. Quite expensive. I spent £2,500 on Roundup. The agent that sold it to me said it's the biggest order he's ever taken for Roundup. Roundup is absorbed by the leaves; it goes down the stem right to the end of the root, and then kills its way back up again, so its a reverse kill. About ten days, especially in the growing period. Couple of weeks in the winter because you've got to wait for the leaves to be dry.

—*Does it leave a residue in the soil?*

No, nothing at all. Gramoxone [or paraquat] will. Gramoxone will kill a man, just a spoonful of it. Having been dealing with sprays for the last forty years, some of them aren't very pleasant – or weren't, but they've been taken off the market. They weren't given enough test. Lethal things. [My son and I] were planting – well it was this field out here, one evening – we were using a pre-emergent spray. It had to be harrowed in immediately behind the sprayer. [My son] was spraying it and I was on another tractor harrowing it in behind him. And the pair of us – our chests next day as tight, tight.... And for a couple of days we weren't very clever. [That spray] was taken off the market. We've been playing with fire quite a few times in the spray-chemical world.

Richard Dudden, 1999.

St Austell Cattle Market

The cattle market in St Austell is still open – but since the following conversation with auctioneer John Blake took place, part of it has been turned into a McDonald's.

People don't take into account the importance of a market. Farmers live a very isolated life. They spend a lot of hours working. There's a lot of one-man-band operations. They come into market, and it gives them a chance to meet their colleagues, talk, discuss their problems, realize they're not the only ones that are having problems. It's very important from a social point of view. Our main opposition is deadweight sales, direct to the abattoir, but of course that is a silent method of selling. You've no idea whether you're doing well or otherwise. Ours is a transparent system. You can see the cattle going across the scale, you see what they weigh, you see what they're making and you know that you've got a similar lot of cattle at home, and they should be worth £X. That's set you targets. Some like to show it off in the ring, which is nice. They worked hard to put it together. It's

St Austell cattle market.

Auctioneer John Blake.

nice for them to go in the ring, and stand up there and be proud of the stock they're selling.

The bidding is very simple, especially here because you're dealing with the same people, week in week out, and you know what they're looking to buy. You know, when you've got a pen of lambs in front of you or you've got a bullock comes in the ring, you know the people that are going to be in contention for that lot. You're concentrating your attention on their expressions.

The selling part is great fun, especially when it's going well. It can get hard when you've got a difficult trade, when the cattle or sheep are not wanted to any degree. You're struggling to attract bids for stock, you're really struggling to get people interested in buying it; then it is hard work.

Early Bed and Breakfast

Diversification started in the thirties on Frank Davey's family farm.

We were a family of five, two boys and three girls. Father wanted to give us a reasonable education and so we went to the Newquay County School for Boys, and my sisters went to Newquay County School for Girls – which incurred a fee. Mother used to take in summer visitors. We would have people come with their families and stay with us for a week or a fortnight. It was usually full board that mother catered for, and sometimes, if the demand was great, we kids would have to go out in one of the barns. We had a camp bed, I remember – and we were tickled.

This was marvellous. We could camp out so that mother could earn this money to help to pay for our education. [The visitors] brought children of our age, so we made a lot of friends back at that time. But the war years – we lost touch with a lot of them, and we didn't bother after the war because the whole system of farming had changed dramatically.

As in the clay industry, new technology was irresistible, but sometimes regrettable.

We were one of the first in our district to have a tractor, and that was in 1931 or '32. When we sold our horses in 1941, we had a sale of seventeen horses of different ages, mares and geldings. They were shire horses. They were beautiful great horses. The shire

Frank Davey driving his tractor with steerage hoe.

horse, lovely horse, full of muscle and strength. I've ploughed with horses. I won first prize in my class with a team of horses and a cock-up plough – I had to stay at home from school for a day to perform with my team. After the ploughing match I showed my team of horses. I took them into the stable and someone helped me to decorate them. Previously I'd been polishing up all the brass etc. – give them a good grooming – and I won the first prize for the best team of horses as well.

The tractor came in, and instead of ploughing an acre a day with two horses I could go out with a tractor and plough ten acres a day, and that was a big saving, especially when your whole industry was tied up with the elements. Weather played such an important part, to get a crop in at the right time.... They say that the difference between a good farmer and a bad farmer is about a fortnight.

Farmwork Past

You know what do make a good farmer? You got to be weak in the head and strong in the arm. This chap used to work for this farmer, and they used to grow a lot of swedes. One day he went out to the field, and there was a little house made of straw. When the farmer got up, 'Dear boy', he said, 'what's in here?' 'I'm in here,' he said – that's the work-chap, you see. [The farmer] said, 'What the hell are 'ee doing with the straw yer?' 'Well', he said, 'It's so bloody cold, I got to make *summat* to get in.' 'Twas bitter cold. Great open farm, right around to the sea, so he made a warm little house for hisself.

WB

Farmwork Past and Present

We bought a little combine in 1957, I think. It was a six-foot cut. Those were baggers in those days. You have someone riding on the combine who bagged it off, [i.e. filled sacks with grain] and then let them down a chute. They fell on the ground. In the evening you had to go round, pick up all the bags. When you were tired at the end of the day, if you had a mass of sacks around the field, and some of them hadn't been tied very well and the strings came undone, or else a mouse had made a hole in the bottom of the bag which you didn't spot, and you had to stuff a bit of straw in the hole....you had to deal with that in the evening. Now, if a farmer's hard put, he can take his trailers out and park them in the field and he can go out by himself with his combine, fill the trailers, go and tip them, go back again. He's a loner. The only living thing he might see all day is the birds, or perhaps a fox or rabbit leaving the corn. He may not speak to anyone until he gets home.

RD

New Methods

New technology, new working methods, new landscape. Frank Davey:

The manufacturers started to produce tractor implements designed for the tractor only. They were wider, and this necessitated... we had to go round and widen all the gateways, because all the gateways were about 6 or 7ft wide, just wide enough to take a horse and cart. We made them up to 8ft wide; then we went up to 10ft wide and later on, moving forward quite a bit, up into the sixties and seventies, we made them 12ft wide – and now on a lot of the farms the gateways are even 14ft wide.

Nearly always the gates were hung with two granite posts that came from the granite quarries here in the county. I can recall, as a young boy, taking a lorry and we drove down to the Penryn granite quarries, and I brought home ten or twelve square granite posts. One would be a fastening post and the other a hanging post. We had to mill them – cut a hole in the post and then either lead in or cement in a crook to hang the gate on – and the other side would be a fastener. The gate would close – we used to call it 'close home', that's an old Cornish word I believe – the gate would strike the fastening post and then there would be a little fastener there to hold the gate.

—When you had to widen the gateways, did you have to enlarge the fields as well?

I suppose we've taken down, on our 500 acre farm, in my lifetime, two miles of hedges. You see, fields were small, specially in a county like Cornwall; fields were very small, because we're a windswept county, and cattle and sheep were all open to the elements.

Walter Bloomfield, lifelong farmer and blunt Cornishman, speaks on holidays.
—Have you ever had a holiday?

One. I went to Ireland for a week. A lot of people go for a holiday, they do go on the beach and all. Well I don't see no bloomin' point leaving home here, sit on a bloody beach for two or three weeks. What's in it? I know you wouldn't do it if you was home, because you'd always find a job to do.

A goat on a Cornish hedge, near Luxulyan.

Jim Knight operating the hose at the Lower Ninestones pit. His nephew, Captain Jim Nicholls, looks on. [WMM]